Editorial Collective
Hillary Lazar
Lara Messersmith-Glavin
Paul Messersmith-Glavin
Maia Ramnath
Theresa Warburton

Production Coordinator
Paul Messersmith-Glavin

Art Direction
Kai Lumumba Barrow
& Gallery of the Streets

Design, Layout, & Printing
Charles Overbeck at Eberhardt Press

Copyeditors
Sam Smith
Kristian Williams

Published by
iAS The Institute for
Anarchist Studies

IAS Board
James Birmingham
Sarah Coffey
Kat Enyeart
Lara Messersmith-Glavin
Paul Messersmith-Glavin
Kristian Williams

IAS Admin
Sara Libby

Institute for Anarchist Studies
PO Box 90454, Portland, OR 97290

E-Mail: PerspectivesOnAnarchistTheory@gmail.com
Web: anarchiststudies.org
Twitter: @iasperspectives
Facebook: www.facebook.com/perspectivesonanarchisttheory

S0-EAX-629

PERSPECTIVES
ON ANARCHIST THEORY
N. 32 || 2021
POWER ISSUE
CONTENTS

Cover art by Kai Lumumba Barrow

Thanks:

Kai Lumumba Barrow; Gallery of the Streets; Erin Bree; Charles at Eberhardt Press; K-Dog and the Twin Cities Workers Defense Alliance; Josh MacPhee of Justseeds Artists' Cooperative; the IAS board, in particular Kristian Williams; the IAS admin, Sara Libby; Kevin Sampsell at Powell's Books; Suzanne, Lorna, and Charles at AK Press; Sam Smith for their expert copyediting assistance; everyone who has donated to and otherwise supported the work of the Institute for Anarchist Studies in this, our 25th year!

ABOUT GALLERY OF THE STREETS AND PAGES FROM THE BOOK OF STUPID...

Gallery of the Streets is a network of autonomous artists, activists, and scholars committed to abolitionist movement-building. Led by queer Black feminist politics, our work is created by people who live, love, fight, work, and play in the margins of racial and gendered capitalism, carceral control, and environmental violences. To learn more about Gallery of the Streets and/or to donate to our work, please check out **galleryofthestreets.org**.

Contributing Artists

Kai Lumumba Barrow
We Begin with Play (cover)

erin bree
Monk's Dream (back cover interior)
Coronascene (136–137)

Koriandre Davenport
Shoe Shine (130–131)

Jazz Franklin
Shoe Code (132–133)

Holly Hardin
On Palms and Bone (118)

Chris Light
I-10 Portal (138–139)
Tree Fighting Capitalism (187)

Kara Lynch AKA Loveyboi as STAR
No Title (104–105)
No Title (134–135)

WHAT HAPPENS WHEN THE POWER GOES OUT
THERESA WARBURTON

WHAT HAS HAPPENED? IN SOME WAYS, THE ANSWER IS SIMPLE because what's happened is the natural progression of a sick society that has forsaken collective stability and health (of all kinds) in favor of power and profit. In other ways, the answer is impossible because what's happened is filtered through a completely surreal existence that, though shared, can somehow still feel incredibly isolating. Having both of these senses at once, of knowing exactly why things have turned out this way while being irreparably shaken by the consequences, has made attending to the question of power feel both important and impossible.

Here at *Perspectives on Anarchist Theory*, we began planning for this issue before COVID or the murder of George Floyd or last year's round of wildfires and hurricanes or the truly punishing election cycle, the outcome of which has simultaneously transformed and solidified many of the things that were written before it. But we conceived of this issue within the structures that made those things possible. In this, the topic of "Power" has felt both the most concrete thing that links these times, places, events, and moods together while also slipping constantly around our minds as we've sought to do the work of bringing this issue into being. Everything we do to collect and share the materials that make up an issue of this journal depends on an infrastructure of resources and relationships. What happens when that infrastructure shakes? What happens when the power goes out?

Every time we turn on a light as dusk comes around, we draw on an infrastructure whose reach and shape are almost unimaginable. It is, to say the least, much bigger than ourselves. But when that power goes out, it can feel like we are left alone. The ways we've learned to move and guide ourselves around a space suddenly shift; different senses give us different directions and we depend on different ways of being to get us through it.

We might find ourselves digging something out of a forgotten drawer or finding that our bodies remember how to do things we rarely practice, like feel our way through a doorway. We might find that our senses adjust to the dark, seeing new shapes and contours or hearing things that are always there but obscured by the constant hum of that infrastructure that has gone out. We might realize suddenly how much we depend on that infrastructure, especially when we get hungry or cold or need to find our way down a treacherous staircase.

But we also find other infrastructures, new and old. We might find new ways to cast light, combine our resources, or huddle together for warmth. We might laugh about what people must have done before power or remind ourselves of the myriad people who live daily without it. We might find old blankets sewn by family or friends who are no longer earthbound, eat foods that we'd forgotten how to savor when the power gave us the ability to do infinite things at once.

So, maybe one way to explain what's happened is that the power has gone out. We felt this in creating this issue, especially as we wrestled with a process that is both creative and constricting. For instance, how do we have deadlines during an ongoing uprising? How do we account for the eroding tensile strength of everyone's physical, mental, and emotional capacities? How do we effectively represent this one moment when the production process stretches out across many months, requiring the careful attention of dozens of people along the way? We spent a long time thinking about how to adjust the infrastructure in ways that accounted for the demands of the moment, both personal and collective, while also making sure that we continued to honor the vision and work that comes with creating a print issue of an anarchist journal.

This process made us see pieces we'd already received in new light, gave us new directions for editing, and new ideas for things to include. It prompted us to draw on other infrastructures to create an online issue of the journal on *Pandemics from the Bottom Up*, which we saw as a way to support authors and ideas that needed to get out more urgently than a print issue could allow. But we also stayed committed to getting this issue into your hands, because the physical object is so much more than only the words. We wanted you to spend time with the prodigious art from Gallery of the Streets, facilitated by Kai Lumumba Barrow, whose work graces our cover. We wanted you to be able to turn a page and put it down while you grabbed another cup of tea. And, most importantly, we wanted to keep supporting the work of independent writers, publishers, artists, and organizers who form the very infrastructure that built the thing in the first place. So, some new infrastructure and some old.

Whether we think of power figuratively, literally, or somewhere in between, perhaps one of the most aphoristic answers to the question of what happens when the power goes out is that "it is better to light a candle than curse the dark." And maybe that's what we've done here. Though, on reflection, it feels like we did our fair share of cursing as well. But also, we spent time becoming more familiar with the nocturnal things, the secreted things, the silent things. When the power went out, we learned to think of the dark differently than needing to be illuminated by the light. Because as we adjust, we see different things: new worlds come about and alive in the darkness. To see darkness as an inherent problem that must be cured by the light (no matter how small) reflects a misunderstanding of the relationship between the two and how power is built into the infrastructure of that balance – to say nothing of the way it ties into the deep-seated denigration of the darkness against the veneration of the light. In this way, we also learned that the darkness is never a natural disaster. And neither are any of the other things our contributors offer here.

It takes new and old strength, new and old knowledge, new and old relationships to remember the infrastructures we already had when we've become dependent on others. It takes just as much work to build new ones. And, it can be tiring, inviting us into the comfort of something known if not trusted and warm if not consoling.

But instead of sleeping when the power goes out, we rise. ▲

AMANDA PRIEBE

THE WORLD IS DYING, DARLING
VERA RUBIN

THE WORLD IS DYING, DARLING. HUMANITY AS WE KNOW IT HAS existed for nearly three hundred thousand years. In that time, only the last 150 years of capitalism has managed to destroy the planet. Clearly there must be a way out of this mess and a way through to a more harmonious world. I am interested in finding the intellectual gaps in rational thought and empirical methodology that can provide solutions to climate change. These gaps can then be added to a Surrealist methodology. This methodology does not claim totality, it is fragmented. This fragmentation allows it flexibility to join many conversations and to add richness, creativity, and a different kind of depth.

There is a profound failure of rational thought. We need to place rational thought historically inside of modernity and capitalism. This is a system of thought rooted in Christian Enlightenment that created rational forms of what is right and what should be common sense. Rationalism, like Christianity, places humans and humanity at the center of its understanding. It does not seek communion with animals and plants as it sees them as something to quantify and to methodologize. It is not concerned with art knowledge unless it is something that can be quantified or justified. Empirical thought posits itself as the most valid knowledge. While of course we need and utilize empirical rational thought, to take it as a truth that exists in a historical vacuum is foolish. Like any form of thought it has its own history of justifying such heinous ideas such as Manifest Destiny, eugenics, trickle-down economics, along with mass production and growth being seen as the measure of health in economics. Rational empirical knowledge strives to lack bias. Hard facts – mathematics and numbers, the scientific method, and the like – have their own political histories and their own social past, present, and futures. Rational methodologies exist in society that shapes them. It is unacceptable to focus solely on rationalism as being the way out of this mess or the best way to understand this mess.

A Surrealist methodology requires a look first at Surrealisms past, the potentiality of the present, and the creative conjecture of the future. Climate change is truly a surreal process in itself. Rational solutions for it often revert back to liberal individualism instead of the collective: electric cars, reusable straws, veganism, etc. While these things are very important and we shouldn't discount the responsibility that the global North has in changing its lifestyle, this simply is not enough.

The imagination of a better world needs to come to the surface. One that decenters humanity and places it in communion with animal knowledges, plant wisdom, mineral language. An interesting experiment is to attempt to get from human centered knowledges to Earth knowledges. Poetry and poetic concepts can serve as a one bridge to non-human and non-cognitive knowledges.

Surrealist methodology must be counter to capitalist logic. Surrealism as an artistic and global phenomena should be approached from an anarchist analysis of this artistic movement. There are plenty of underlying concepts of political Surrealism and a history of Surrealism in combating white supremacy and imperialism. A foundation of a Surrealist methodology must understand race as a political category that seeks to destabilize and decenter whiteness.

The limits of political Surrealism lie in Western European Continental thinking. Continental thinking sees thoughts and strategies as total, whole, and applicable everywhere. Continental thinking should be replaced with island and archipelago thinking. Caribbean philosopher and Surrealist Eduard Glissant looks at the potential of seeing the archipelago as a connection to many disparate tendencies and potentialities. Continental becomes imperialism while the islands become ripe with multiple connections. Glissant posits replacing rational concepts with poetic concepts also known as poecepts. Thus Surrealism becomes not just a way of drawing poetic parallels but a way of looking at poetic formation of new knowledges.

The use of the exquisite corpse is one approach in a Surrealist methodology. An exquisite corpse is an intuitive collective drawing done in pieces. One person will draw a picture, fold it over and the next person creates the next image, and the process repeats. I want to abstract an understanding of the exquisite corpse to seeing parts of a picture where the creation before and after is not known. To look at how creating such a collective form of art can also be used to look at nature and animals. The exquisite corpse becomes a piece of codevelopment. We are in an evolutionary codevelopment with other animals and plants. Our destinies are linked, which is a true challenge to liberal individualism and capitalism.

Donna Haraway speaks of the power of "SF:" science fiction, speculative feminism. We should add a new SF: Surrealist Fantasies. How can we use the exquisite corpse as a method of critique? We can use plant knowledge to connect the interstellar with the terrestrial. The dream states of plants in their connection to the universe is an interesting departure of what can be learned from dark matter and parallel realities. The dream states that exist within all of us have this potentiality to imagine new improvisational solutions.

Many cities across the globe are using improvisation to deal with the ravages of capital. In Lagos, Nigeria people are able to reconstitute their cities' landscapes with little planning and the movement of garbage into essential structures of living. The lessons of improvisation from the Global South must be heard and understood by the Global North. The best way to do this and exchange this knowledge is with open borders. Improvisation and intuitive automatic writings are a foundation of a Surrealist practice. To put that into action requires destabilizing Western knowledge and the hubris of neoliberalism.

Finally, Surrealist mysticisms can unleash non-narrative knowledges, extinct knowledges, and native/non-white knowledges by using symbol and myth. There are plenty of pitfalls with this, one being that a Surrealist methodology has the ability to whiten and appropriate oppressed peoples' knowledges to make them more palatable to the Global North. However, mysticism can allow us to be connected to so many modes of being. Plant medicines have their own poetry. Totem animals have their powers. The mysticism, extinct knowledges, and the occult can connect us with the non-rational and provide even more solutions to healing a wrecked world.

Seeing an approach of Surrealism using poetry, the exquisite corpse, automatic and intuitive writing, improvisation, and mysticism can lead us not only to creative solutions but provide us with the tools of decentering whiteness and liberal rational thought. I can only hope and pray for collective solutions for all of us to stay with the trouble we have gotten ourselves into. Ⓐ

Catherine Marr (Vera Rubin) lives in Joshua Tree, CA. She is a visual artist, DJ, autodidact, life-long revolutionary, and writer. She is working on her masters at European Graduate School in Valletta, Malta working on topics of surrealism, climate change, revolution, and animal communion. Her musical selections of post punk, left field, and techno can be found at soundcloud.com/verarubin and on instagram at @surrealist_fantasies.

WE STAND IN SOLIDARITY WITH

FREEDOM FIGHTERS OF ROJAVA

LIVING YOUR LIFE IN A STATE OF WAR

SHANE BURLEY

IN COUNTERINSURGENCIES OF THE PAST, REVOLUTIONARY MOVEMENTS have been undone through a combination of ideology, propaganda, and expropriation; in recent years, however, Turkey has dispensed with such liberal forms of coercion. Maybe it is the Trump effect (and the Alternative for Germany effect, and the Freedom Party of Austria effect, and so on) that gives Turkey's president, Recep Tayyip Erdoğan, the freedom to cut the bullshit and simply brutalize the autonomous region of northeastern Syria. They have dropped the pretense of consented governance and replaced it with the most modern of genocidal tools: white phosphorous.

After Trump decided to pull US troops out of the Syrian conflict, Turkey did as we expected they would. Using proxy forces in the form of Jihadi rebels, as well as constant air raids, Turkey escalated its decades-long war on the Kurdistan Region. What has been established in Rojava since the state receded amid the Syrian Civil War in 2012–2013 is no less than the early blossoms of a revolutionary society. The principle of *democratic confederalism* is in effect: an idea introduced by Kurdistan Workers' Party (PKK) leader Abdullah Öcalan, who synthesized a new approach to politics inspired, in part, by American anarchist Murray Bookchin, along with the community councils that have long been a part of Kurdish culture. What we see here is a society in transition: one that is trying to move away from entrenched patriarchy, through the intentional enfranchisement of women; away from neoliberal capitalism, through the empowerment of cooperatives and communal resource development; and toward a society run through direct democratic structures. All of these efforts remain in flux; they are, as with any revolution in process, still finding themselves.

The significance of this cannot be, and has not been, ignored: we are watching an anarchist vision (of some sort) take place in the real world. The importance of this moment is also evinced by the increasingly authoritarian political offices of Turkey. The revolutionary changes occurred in the three autonomous cantons of northeastern Syria, but they are now being compressed on all sides as Turkey uses war crimes to destabilize the region, the Kurds have been forced back into an alliance with Assad, and Russia and the United States continue to engage in an international blunder. A revolutionary society has become a revolutionary moment – one that could remain temporally fixed since this experiment could come to a brutal end amid carpet bombings.

"It is not only the invasion, of course, which has already claimed [the] lives of hundreds of civilians and displaced more than 3,000,000. It is the world of nation-states involved in the so-called Astana process," says Andrej Grubačić, a sociologist and organizer originally from the Balkans who has been active in Rojava solidarity, including as a university professor in the region.

> Turkish invasion, paradoxically enough, is creating the possibility for completion of an old Assadist dream, one of the so-called Arab belt, a project that was initiated in [the] 1960s. This project of demographic engineering, of breaking the Kurdish majority, was never complete, but I am afraid that it now might become a reality. Between wars and processes of turkification and arabization, of breaking the democratic autonomy, confederalism of Rojava is in danger of becoming "statified."[1]

A host of autonomous structures have emerged in Rojava, including experiments in transformative justice, women's empowerment, communal economic democracies; thus it is an entire future of alternatives that is jeopardized by the military attacks. The choices they have are now to collaborate with previous enemies or face extermination, which could decidedly end that autonomy and return Kurdistan to the status of contested quasi-states. And that is one of the best-case scenarios.

So, the question that many on the international left are asking, particularly in the United States, is: Did we miss it? Is this a story, like the Spanish Revolution, about which anarchists will write piles of books? Is Rojava merely a brief window into a future foreclosed? Is it a reminder of what could be, but is not yet possible, or is it something we are living through in real time?

Revolutionary politics lives in people through the intoxicating effect of massive ideas. These fantasies, visions of what could be possible, are enough to sustain entire social movements, entire lifetimes in organizing. This spark seems small – it lives largely in our imagination – but we are nevertheless seduced by its power to see something much larger (a small key opens a large door).[2] For most of us, however, it is only in the briefest of moments that those ideas are put into action: the prefiguration of a new world that we see in a social movement or community space. They never expand to a whole

A host of autonomous structures have emerged in Rojava, including experiments in transformative justice, women's empowerment, communal economic democracies...

society. The idea itself has to be enough – with the seeming possibility to become real if the stars aligned (or if we were simply capable enough). Only in a few instances have these ideas been realized at a society-wide level, and Rojava has been one of the largest; three million people in a country-sized land zone, establishing decentralized direct democracy in almost every area of social life, with the buy-in of almost the entire community. It sounds like a leftist fever dream, or the projection of utopian revisionism on foreign space, yet even the most cynical have had to rethink their dismissals.

The story of the Kurdish geographic region (and people) is one of starts and stops, persistence in the aftermath of seeming total loss. The Kurdish ethnic group is dispersed across a number of countries, including Turkey, Syria, and Iraq, and it has been fighting for an established state of its own for over a hundred years. Snapshots of Kurdish autonomy have collided with nationalisms of neighbors, who have reacted with ferocious repression and ethnic cleansing.

In 1984 the Kurdistan Workers' Party (PKK) underwent a shift from what began as largely a student movement in the 1970s to a Marxist-Leninist paramilitary organization that fought with the Turkish state in a protracted guerilla war, operating from the relative safety of the mountains.[3] The goal was national liberation through a socialist Kurdistan. After the PKK's leader, Abdullah Öcalan, was captured and imprisoned in 1999 at a single-person island facility, he began to shift the ideological orientation of the movement in the libertarian direction. Öcalan's writings, which ultimately changed the entire outlook of the PKK, advocate for democratic confederalism, an egalitarian social system that rejects a state in favor of direct democratic community control and a rethinking of all of the dominating institutions of the society that came before. This takes the form of regional councils that prioritize the participation of women, the collectivization of resources (while rejecting coercive acquisition), a focus on transformative justice, and the use of Bookchin's idea of social ecology as a means to repair the environmental destruction of the region wrought by resource extraction.

Thus, all aspects of society are up for reinterpretation, from the role of women to relationships with the natural world. This is a revolutionary situation: an entirely new type of civilization is forming, in spite of crushing chaos surrounding it.

Internationale

There is an argument favored by angry parts of the left that Rojava, with its brief moments of tacit support from the United States, lacks the character of a true revolution. Instead, the Western left is accused of projecting its fantasies, seeing what it wants to see in Rojava, and trekking to its cantons to play revolution. Part of the reason that line fails is the fact that Rojava has been an international project from the beginning. Öcalan had reached out to Murray Bookchin for counsel before Bookchin's death, and he has built relationships with his daughter, Debbie Bookchin, as well as the Institute for Social Ecology, of which Bookchin was a founder. This has helped to create an ideological interplay between the cantons and the worldwide movement toward ground-up democracy, whether it calls itself anarchism or not. Projects like Symbiosis, which includes the Libertarian Socialist Caucus of the Democratic Socialists of America (which is larger than any other anarchist organization in the US), Cooperation Jackson from Mississippi, and the Asamblea de los Pueblos Indígenas del Istmo en Defensa de la Tierra y el Territorio (APOODTT), members of the Binniza indigenous community of Gui 'Xhi' Ro' who have kicked the Mexican state out of their village.

People from around the world were invited to Rojava, not just to bear witness (though that was encouraged), but to participate in autonomous projects that were a part of its democratic structure. One of these is the Internationalist Commune of Rojava, which began in 2017 in association with the Rojava Youth Movement (YCR) and built itself

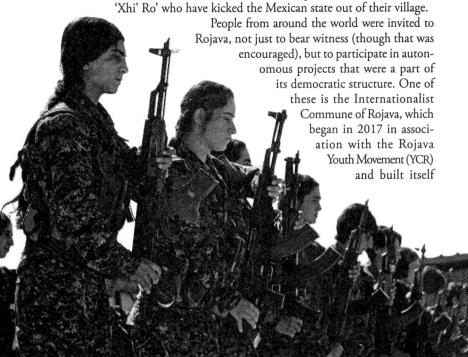

around the principle "Learn, support, organize." This has resulted in a number of campaigns, such as an international educational academy and "Make Rojava green again," a project that has brought widespread interest, due to its use of the principles of Bookchin's social ecology as an answer to colonialist resource harvesting.

Anarchists and socialists from around the world signed up as volunteers, many joining the International Freedom Battalion (IFB), which was modeled on the Abraham Lincoln Brigade.

"Rojava is not a museum where the revolution can be examined and measured. Rojava is not a monument of past battles. Rojava is a living and developing organism. And those who approach it as revolutionaries become part of it," says the Commune to prospective recruits. Volunteers are required to commit to at least six months of work, often sleep on floors, and must learn the local Kurmancî dialect. The Commune is not interested in tourism; they want committed participation. The Commune has earned it an official place in the confederal structure of Rojava, which is to say that it is a very real part of the revolutionary society rather than just a collection of politicized transplants.

A different version of this was the support provided by volunteers to the militant effort fought by both the People's Protection Units (YPG) and the Women's Protection Units (YPJ) in the fight against the Daesh (ISIS) forces. Anarchists and socialists from around the world signed up as volunteers, many joining the International Freedom Battalion (IFB), which was modeled on the Abraham Lincoln Brigade that brought volunteers to aid the anarchists of the Confederación Nacional del Trabajo (CNT) and Federación Anarquista Ibérica (FAI) against the nationalist forces of Francisco Franco. The comparison is well made; indeed, the situation is strikingly similar, as it brought in confederated battalions from Turkey like the Communist Labor Party of Turkey/Leninist and United Freedom Forces (BÖG), whose participation in the conflict could have dire consequences, given that their home country considers participation in the fight a form of material aid to declared terrorist organizations (the PKK and Democratic Union Party of Syria).

Another volunteer company was the International Revolutionary People's Guerrilla Forces (IRPGF), an explicitly anarchist militia that joined in the fighting with recruits from around the world. In a pamphlet, they wrote:

> Our role is two-fold; to be an armed force capable of defending liberatory social revolutions around the world while simultaneously being a force capable of

insurrection and struggle against all kyriarchal forms of power wherever they exist. We do not enter conflict zones with intent to command but rather, while retaining our autonomy as a collective, to fight alongside other armed groups in solidarity with those who are oppressed, exploited, and facing annihilation.[4]

These organizations sought common cause, collaborating in the ongoing military struggle against ISIS, sometimes alongside the Syrian Democratic Forces (SDF), sometimes in direct military command. They acted in solidarity in their support of the Rojava project, the destruction of ISIS fascist forces, and the freedom for the Kurdish people from persecution. Likewise, what protection they could afford Rojava was a direct result of the global solidarity effort that helped to influence the decisions of those around them. The region has faced decades of economic blocks, underdevelopment, and hyper-exploitation, alongside attacks from Turkey (not to mention Syria and Iraq, among others), so the creation of an external movement acting in solidarity was critical. It was also never viewed as a form of charity, because people around the world saw Rojava as a crack in neoliberalism and statecraft. And since the people in Rojava agreed with this perception, it was possible to forge a symbiotic relationship between those building a new society on the inside and those trying their best to defend it from the outside. Supporting Rojava's revolution was not a separate struggle from the organizing that happened back at home, they were the same battle just happening in different locations. Through their provision of support, and sincere participation, the people of Rojava fostered an internationalism with the potency to launch revolutionary politics on a global scale.

We Assume We Will Lose

As the bombs began to drop on Afrin, many reacted as if this international, collaborative project was merely a memory, dashed by US betrayal and the nationalist war machine of Turkey, or perhaps something that happened "out there" rather than being within our grasp.

"I think that the incredible strides that the Kurds have made in achieving a society that is feminist, egalitarian, non-sectarian, ecological, is such an extraordinary accomplishment and provides such a unique model, in particular in direct democracy, that it is something that everyone who, again, considers themselves a progressive or an activists should seek to preserve," said Debbie Bookchin, who was doing international solidarity work for the region, when I spoke with her in November of 2019.

> [We should] also look to [Rojava] as a model of how we can build a social movement in this country that actually goes beyond protest and beyond voting for a

good Democratic Socialist candidate, and starts to really empower people on the local level. And the Kurds have shown us *exactly* how this can be done. By creating local assemblies, assembly democracy where power is devolved to the local level. Where politics is re-invented. Where politics is not something that is done by a professional class who you have to put your faith in and hope they do the right thing or make the right decision, but politics is a thing which is done by ordinary people in their everyday lives who build a dual power, a new society within the shell of the old.[5]

The reality is that the Rojava revolution could be summarily destroyed, at least in the form we know it now, by any of a range of intrusions. Turkey's brutality has continued to escalate as constant shelling kills civilians in the hundreds and thousands, and the conflict has already led to the internal displacement of more than four hundred thousand Kurds. Because the United States has left the Kurds so vulnerable, they have been forced to turn to an earlier enemy, Assad's untrained military forces, for support; thus they have returned to the very Ba'athist fold that has historically rejected Kurdish autonomy. And all of these: economic starvation, mass killings, stratification as a solution to increased instability, are eschatological. Each factor works in concert with the other to suggest that this moment of Rojava's revolution is only for a moment: a brief glimmer before the rest of the world collapses onto it with the weight of our circumstances.

So, there is desperation when we talk of Rojava, when we tell stories of the crimes against the people, and, even more profoundly, when we talk of their victories. Yet the deep well of sadness that attends this conversation forgets one key fact: the situation was always dire, always uncertain, always stacked against them.

A War Society

Rojava is a society set in one of the most traditional molds for revolutionary communities, birthed in struggle against the far right and the austerities of capital. The revolution did not emerge out of the best of times, nor out of a series of social democratic reforms that leveled the playing field, or via social movements piles of money and resources. It emerged, by any measure, from some of the worst moments, in the midst of a three-way fight between the neighboring states, with the fascist insurgency of ISIS amassing on all sides.[6]

The most cogent previous example of this dynamic was the Spanish Revolution, where such instability in effect enabled the anarchists of Catalonia, Andalusia, Valencia, and Aragon the autonomy to collectivize agriculture and industry. The Spanish Republic was formed in

1931 in a progressive turn from the years of monarchical rule, and in the subsequent years a turbulent modernization campaign pushed toward addressing the economic crisis in the country. As the Popular Front coalition of left-wing electoralists took the elections in 1936, and the anarchists with the CNT-FAI in the north were building strength, a fascist coup plunged the country into civil war as the propertied classes backed reactionary Catholic monarchism. Amid this chaos, with fighting on all sides, we could witness anarcho-syndicalism becoming more than an idea. The anarchists ran factories collectively and created communal farming systems; everything in society was on the table for restructuring, reimaging, or abolition. The anarchists eventually lost, in part due to Soviet betrayal, and Franco would determine the direction of Spain for the next forty years. Nevertheless, for a moment, a whole new world of limitless possibilities existed.[7]

A similar example is the Ukranian Free Territory during the Ukranian revolution of 1917–1921. The Revolutionary Insurrectionary Army of Ukraine, led by anarchist Nestor Makhno (the ideological progenitor of the so-called platformist tendency in anarchism) protected what were referred to as "free soviets," decentralized collectives operated along libertarian communist principles. This was, again, a period of civil war and social revolution, in which the "White Army" of the Russian czar engaged in protracted battle against the Red Army, along with the anarchists who joined the fight (who adopted a more hands-off approach than that of the Bolsheviks). Once the White Army was defeated, the Soviets turned on the anarchists and crushed their burgeoning society, leaving us with nothing more than a flash that has stayed with social movements as both a blueprint and a portrait.

Our history is filled with such examples. The May 1968 student uprisings in France, which took over urban space and tried to reconstruct our communities, with Situationism behind their eyes, all done amid austerity, rather than affluence. The Argentinian factory recuperation movement of the early 2000s coincided with massive economic collapse and job loss, which helped to lead the takeovers out of necessity rather than just cold ideology. The Cascadia "free territory" was created in Oregon in 1995 as activists outside Eugene fought against a timber sale of ancient forests, creating a protest camp that became, during a year-long siege, a community of its own, out of reach by the state.[8] Even the Zapatista uprising in 1994 is a direct result of the economic assault of the North American Free Trade Agreement (NAFTA), along with the Mexican state's repression of southern indigenous sovereignty and self-determination.[9]

When we say that Rojava is a revolutionary society, we mean it quite literally. It is a war society. One that exists, as we know it now, in the eye of the storm, building a utopian vision surrounded by encroaching violence. It is a future world that exists under threat, that has never

existed outside of that danger. There has never been a moment when the Rojava experiment was safe; there was no time when it was guaranteed the right to see through its vision. The ideas that the PYD and PKK brought into the cantons were the result of decades of guerilla war in the mountains of Turkey, a fight for a Kurdish independence that existed as a kind of speculative fiction.

Like in Spain and Ukraine, the disappearance of much of the Syrian state amid a crushing wave of genocidal bloodshed created a window, a moment, when its absence allowed for another series of experiments to fill the vacuum. This vision was further forged in the battle against ISIS, an antifascist revolutionary act against a theocratic authoritarian insurgency, and this helped to create international bonds through the anarchist militias, the International Freedom Battalion, and press darlings like the Lions of Rojava. Struggle is the heart of the vision for Rojava, the story it tells about itself. It is an idealism that comes from a living experience of oppression, and every moment of Rojava's existence has been built on struggle, the wars from which it emerged, and its own internal fight to remake itself while confronting the oppressions in its own society (and all others as well). Rojava is at war, it has always been at war.

The Danger of Remaking the World

We start revolutions not because they are easy, but because they are hard. The easy path would be to continue with some version of the status quo, to find reforms that make sense, and that can move us toward improvements. Revolutions are risky. They usually fail, and even when they don't, a lot of heartache and trials lie ahead. History is not linear, with determined end points, but rather a caustic racket of explosive moments of change (or cycles of contention): 1871, 1917, 1936, 1968, 1980, 1989, 1994, 2011, 2013, 2020, and a lot of others in between. A revolutionary society wants more than we have had before, more than has ever seemed possible to grasp. And so, we make the choice to fight for something, to suffer and sacrifice, because we want to roll the dice. Because we want more.

Revolutions exist inside of the passion of a life worth living, one where comfort and stability are sacrificed for the visceral feeling that comes when every decision holds the weight of the world. In Rojava, every moment matters: even seemingly mundane parts of society are imbued with meaning, because they are at war, not only with the invading armies but also with their own past. The ways armies are trained, bridges are built, and food is grown are all on the table; all is being reimagined, and all are areas of struggle.

> **History is not linear, with determined end points, but rather a caustic racket of explosive moments of change.**

A revolutionary society is expected to have pushback, because if the revolution goes viral, it becomes a direct threat to power. One cannot expect such a society, which exists by virtue of taking back property and resources, to be granted amnesty by those who legally owned them before.

"Everybody I spoke to had a very revolutionary sentiment. It's just a horrendously difficult situation. As it always will be [in a revolution], it was what I realized when I was there," Dr. George Hagglnud, who had just gotten back from a medical convoy in Tel Temir in Rojava, told me in late 2019. Hagglnud reflected on the difficulty that pushing for these kinds of revolutionary changes would always happen, not just in Rojava's particular context, but anytime the transformations happening are this profound.

> If we do the same thing on the West Coast, do you think it's going to be easy? Do you think the rest of the world is going to support us? Send us weapons and applaud us? No, it's going to be the exact same situation. It's going to be like Republican Spain. They're going to embargo

you. They're going to refuse to send you weapons, but arm the other side. The exact same situation as what we're seeing in Rojava. And, of course that's difficult. And, of course, that makes a revolution complicated. But the people said that they expect dark times ahead, but they are not prepared to give up their self-governance.[10]

The fight to defend oneself and one's community is in itself part of a process of liberation; revolutionary self-defense is a new understanding of what security and self-determination means. The Internal Security Forces of Rojava (Asayish) would beg you not to call them police. They provide community-protection services, and those who serve have to learn nonviolent conflict resolution skills and feminist theory before they can even think of picking up a gun. In the future, they hope to offer Asayish training to everyone, breaking down the need for a professionalized class of law keepers and bringing it over to everyone in collaboration. They are even implementing transformative justice approaches to harm in support of the vision of eliminating the carceral state. When this threat has ended though, the weight of capital and imperialism will continue to loom, as will conditions of scarcity, sectarian conflicts, and social conditioning. Struggle will continue because that is the very meaning of a revolution. There is no end in sight.

"For believe me! – the secret for harvesting from existence the greatest fruitfulness and the greatest enjoyment is: to live dangerously!" said Friedrich Nietzsche in *The Gay Science*, resting on the notion that it is only under strife that we become our best selves.

> Build your cities on the slopes of Vesuvius! Send your ships into uncharted seas! Live at war with your peers and yourselves! Be robbers and conquerors as long as you cannot be rulers and possessors, you seekers of knowledge! Soon the age will be past when you could be content to live hidden in forests like shy deer! At long last the search for knowledge will reach out for its due: – it will want to rule and possess, and you with it![11]

This logic has been applied in countless superficial excuses for persecution and unnecessary endurance, but what if we can rethink its context? What if the shadow of the mountain is simply the realization of the battle that is in front of us – one that is inescapable if we want to move the immovable? The challenge of Rojava is inevitable, because it is in direct proportion to what it has set out to accomplish: nothing less than rewriting the rules of civilization. Of course, it will be an uphill battle. To acknowledge this fact is not to give cover to the nations (and Jihadi terrorists) who are encroaching on the cantons. These are the culmination of international betrayals that have the ability to completely obliterate what they have built, to end the experiment before it becomes the status quo. The war that cracked a window for the revolution may be the same one that invites its messy end, almost as though the world was promised a temporary landscape from which to make their future work.

It is an open question as to whether or not a new world can be birthed without a massive conflict that destabilizes the old, but there is no debate as to whether or not war is required to change ourselves. Each piece of the society around us, every horror and dream, is reflected inside us as well. To build something wholly new requires tearing the roots from the earth, to build new buildings and new arrangements and new identities and new understandings of ourselves. A war

The challenge of Rojava is inevitable, because it is in direct proportion to what it has set out to accomplish: nothing less than rewriting the rules of civilization.

society is defined not only by its literal military clashes, but by what happens when we are forced to live without stasis and to let that moment of flux be hopeful, rather than one of only tension and anxiety. To make war is to absolve ourselves of stasis, to say that the safety of the status quo is no longer worth it, and to instead attack the foundations of what we have known with the hope that we can rebuild something greater.

According to Berivan Qerecox, who works with the Women Defend Rojava campaign from Kongra Star in Kobanî,

> [W]hat is happening before our eyes is clearly an attempt at ethnic cleansing and an attempt at stopping the society here from existing. Whatever they say, whatever they pay lip service to, the fascist Turkish state's goals are nothing less than that … In one sense there is a very real and very immediate threat. In another sense, I do think it's important to understand that the experiment here and the project here is much, much wider than just about one place or about some land and not something that could just be destroyed overnight. It is not tied to certain seats of power that you could just come and destroy and bomb and then the organization will, in itself, be gone. The real meaning, the real heart and soul of what is happening here, is about people day to day, dedicating themselves to working hard to reimagining how human beings relate to each other and how we create the systems we live under. And you can't just stop those people doing that overnight. And in the future that might look very different, but these values have lasted a really long time. They were around before the autonomous administration was able to take

the space, to build the structures of self-organizations in Northeastern Syria. And they will be around for a really long time in whatever form the future takes.[12]

The gravity of the situation can be a call to action, rather than a sign that all is lost. The revolution runs deeper into the legacy of Kurdish resistance and what it means for the rest of us. If we give up now, then this will only have been a window into what could have been, a story we will continue to tell for the coming decades in reading groups or at conferences or in our own personal laments and revolutionary longings. We have lived with so many windows into these revolutionary possibilities (after all, we still remember Catalonia), but there is a need to crack this one open so that it becomes the future. We don't just want another moment in time. And we can do that: not just by acting in solidarity and support, but by living our lives in a state of war. This means to commit to the same struggle, not just through the romanticization of a fight thousands of miles away, but by engaging in the here and now as a single global project. There is nothing inevitable about the collapse of Rojava, because there is nothing inevitable about the world in which we live. We move it daily, and we can build something awe inspiring, or we can let it burn. The very real nightmare of Turkish attacks – and the unlikelihood of building a new world in the shell of the old – should never dissuade us of our hopes. It was always unlikely that the imaginary could actually be real. And it certainly was always a war zone.

Bring the War Home

What the people in Rojava want, as they have said over and over again, is to bring the ideas of democratic confederalism to the rest of the world. The greatest act of solidarity is to organize at home, to confederate globally, to challenge power, capitalism, and the state, and thereby make a new world possible.

The philosopher Michael Hardt has a famous story about this, one he retells while rowing a boat through Central Park in the 2008 documentary *An Examined Life*. In the 1980s he was a part of a procession of young leftist students and radicals who traveled to Central America to try and support the revolutionary movements, such as the Sandinistas and uprisings in El Salvador. I also remember stories recalled by older organizers, when I first organized, about how they went and picked coffee for a year under the idea that their presence might stop American-backed militias (spoiler alert: it didn't). While the people appreciated the support, what they really wanted was their American comrades to go home and make revolution, since, in reality, if the insurgencies were ever successful they would still be crushed by the might of American imperialism and global capitalism.

The reality is that Rojava can only serve as a window when it is the only revolutionary society on the map. There can be no "anarchism in one country"; this is a global system with international consequences, and the eyes of the rich are watching. The most important act of solidarity is to make their struggle, which is to create a wholly new society, our own. This is what can be done to make the confederation more than a passing stage, and that means getting to know your neighbors, creating projects that matter, and investing a real stake in your community.

According to Debbie Bookchin, the lessons of Rojava can be applied at home can be applied at home by reinventing politics and instituting dual power, which she suggests, includes

> not only the things that have already been done on multiple levels successfully by the left like creating alternative educational institutions or co-ops or tenants' rights organizations, but also getting involved politically at the local level to send people into city councils so they can further use that position to further strengthen the local assemblies so that we really give people a sense of empowerment and create a sense of community and build a society based on mutual aid and cooperation.[13]

This is, in essence, to bring Rojava's successes within reach in other countries. This would have to also come with a commitment to struggle, to build connections that extend, like tributaries, across communities; to meet people where they are at; to locate the problems and build solutions; and to know each other and have a stake in one another's survival. It won't be easy. There is no promise that we will be successful. And the stakes are incredibly high. While the society in the cantons emerged within a particular warscape, the terrain of conflict is far larger, and it extends beyond borders and into our own lives. So, to commit to that war is to commit to the life that comes by way of this crisis of civility: not merely to recognize the battle as tragedy, but rather to embrace life amid the conflict that arises when we fight for each other. Revolutions occur as cracks in the surface as pressure mounts, and this is increasingly the day-to-day reality of life in a society of crumbling infrastructure, disaster capitalism, and mass extinction.

We live in a war society already. Let's do it differently this time. Ⓐ

Shane Burley is a writer and filmmaker based in Portland, Oregon. He is the author of Fascism Today: What It Is and How to End It *(AK Press) and is currently editing* No Pasaran, *a collection of essays on fascism and antifascism for the IAS and AK Press. His work has appeared in places such as* In These Times, Waging Nonviolence, Labor Notes, ROAR Magazine, Perspectives, *and* Upping the Anti. *Follow him on Twitter:* @shane_burley1.

Notes

1 Andrej Gubračić, Interview with Shane Burley, November 11, 2019.

2 Reference to Strangers in a Tangled Wilderness, ed., *A Small Key Can Open A Large Door: The Rojava Revolution* (Oakland: AK Press, 2015).

3 The organization's origins date to 1978, but the years of armed struggle in the Qandil Mountains began in 1984.

4 International Revolutionary People's Guerrilla Forces, *The Struggle Continues: Positions of the IRPGF,* available at https://usa.anarchistlibraries.net/library/international-revolutionary-people-s-guerrilla-forces-the-struggle-continues (accessed November 18, 2020).

5 Debbie Bookchin, Interview by Shane Burley, November 6, 2019.

6 Michael Staudenmaier and Rami El-Amine, "The Three Way Fight," *Upping the Anti,* no. 5, November 19, 2009, available at: https://uppingtheanti.org/journal/article/05-the-three-way-fight-debate (accessed November 18, 2020).

7 Murray Bookchin, *To Remember Spain: The Anarchist and Syndicalist Revolution of 1936* (Oakland: AK Press, 2001); Frank Mintz, *Anarchism and Workers' Self-Management in Revolutionary Spain* (Oakland: AK Press, 2013); Danny Evans, *Revolution and the State: Anarchism in the Spanish Civil War, 1936–1939* (Chico: AK Press, 2020).

8 Tim Ream, dir., *Pickaxe* (1999; CrimethInc.).

9 Mihalis Mentinis, *Zapatistas: The Chiapas Revolt and What It Means for Radical Politics* (London: Pluto Press, 2006).

10 George Hagglnud, Interview with Shane Burley, October 31, 2019.

11 Friedrich Nietzsche, *The Gay Science* (New York: Random House, 1974).

12 Berivan Qerecox, Interview with Shane Burley, November 3, 2019.

13 Debbie Bookchin, Interview with Shane Burley, November 6, 2019.

BUILDING ONLINE POWER

CAYDEN MAK

MARK ZUCKERBERG, THE CEO OF FACEBOOK, LIKES TO CLAIM THAT HIS company's goal is to bring all the world's people closer together through networking. That's a truly astounding fiction, as Facebook – and effectively all of the firms dominating the internet today – are motivated to capture all of human experience as "behavior" from which they can extract value in order to sell more advertising.

But what if the internet wasn't just a medium for extracting the raw materials of this new means of production? What if we treated the internet seriously as a place – a location where people spend their work and leisure time, not just in transit, but in community? There is more than one way to do politics and build a community on the internet, and in spite of the current dominance of surveillance capitalism as the model for governing the web, it is not the logical conclusion of the technology itself. Rather, it's the consequence of social, political, economic, and legal processes, as Shoshana Zuboff argues in *The Age of Surveillance Capitalism*.[1]

The internet as we experience it is a designed system that is itself the result of systems of power that are much older, and perhaps less visible, than it is. Therefore, it is possible – and necessary – to contest for power online. However, our existing models for online organizing are heavily focused on mass mobilization, utilizing the web as a communications medium connecting interested individuals to organizations and one another.

At 18 Million Rising, we've been at the forefront of trying to figure out how to move away from the mass mobilization/communications model of online organizing and toward models that foreground humans and, hopefully, help foster a different kind of internet. Founded as an organization specializing in mass mobilization through email and petitions, we've evolved to include a variety of other tactics while keeping those tools in our toolbox for strategic moments. We primarily organize young Asian Americans, a group of people more heavily online than any other race/age demographic, and for whom belonging may be particularly elusive. Our generation, often stuck between the home cultures of our parents and their homelands and the popular and political culture of the United States, frequently struggles to find belonging offline.

To make matters more complex, the term "Asian American," in the popular imagination, spans a universe of stereotypes that young Asian Americans often feel at war with. The origins of the term, of course, are in the Third World Liberation Front, when Asian American organizers were on the hunt for a descriptor that felt new, fresh, and relevant to the political work they were undertaking. Since the 70s, the term has been defanged and turned into an almost meaninglessly general census category. Also since the 70s, who *might* count as Asian Americans has been shaped by U.S. imperialism, immigration policy, and globalization, making potential members more diverse, and dividable, than ever before.

18MR's work is particularly urgent because of the ways the social and economic pressures placed on our generation are separating them from other communities. We're more likely to have moved to cities away from our families of origin for work. We're often burdened with heavy debt, while at the same time serving as the young professional or creative vanguard of gentrification in cities across the continent. We've watched our civil liberties be eroded by the expanding national security apparatus after 9/11. While young Asian Americans trend leftward, it's by no means a given that we will be full-throated participants in social movements. And there is an expanding counterweight: the rise of right-wing movements both in our nations of origin and in the United States point to the growing possibility many of our people will be recruited away.

We found, starting very early on, that the people we were most trying to reach were tech savvy and highly skeptical. They were critical and thoughtful, often seeing through the somewhat manipulative clickbait tactics popular at the time, and which still reign in certain digital programs. They were asking earnest questions about what it means to be Asian American – and demonstrated time and time again that they wanted a political home that could host difficult conversations about our role in movements for racial, economic, gender, and environmental justice. We upped our game because we saw those early indicators, and it means our work continues to be robust, relevant, and incisive nearly eight years on.

Five Questions to Use the Internet for Power

These five questions – which I return to on a weekly basis to inform our strategy and tactics – are necessary but not sufficient for the task of treating the internet as a true place. I hope you'll find them useful in your organizing.

Question One:
What principles guide our work online?

Developing a set of shared principles may seem straightforward, but it's critical. There are some tensions that are worth articulating here that we've encountered in developing our own operating principles. While they certainly aren't unique to the internet, the way that people use the internet often amplifies these tensions in our day-to-day work.

In particular, there is a tension between rigidity and flexibility. One of the greatest challenges of building a comprehensive organizing strategy for the internet is the sheer speed and volume of information and interaction. Being clear about what your principles are, while articulating them with the flexibility to respond to a swiftly changing landscape, is vital to being able to make decisions in alignment with your principles in the first place. On the other hand, principles that aren't rooted, that you cannot articulate in alignment with a broader radical tradition, don't serve as bulwarks against the pull of trends or fads.

A strong set of principles can guide your political formation through tricky questions of what tools to use and why; how to respond to punctuated moments of collective grief, rage, or joy; and keep the collective on track when defining who "your people" are. 18 Million Rising's operating principles articulate a clear politics of collective action in the service of our anti-racist, anti-capitalist, and anti-imperialist analysis that also complicates our relationship with technology itself. While the internet is critical for *how* we do our work, the people remain *why* – fetishizing the tools takes us further from our why. Getting clear, and staying clear, even when the waters you're navigating are murky, builds trust and allows you to engage in principled struggle within your team and more publicly with others.

Question Two:
Who do we need on our team so we can co-create a transdisciplinary strategy?

We intentionally don't run 18 Million Rising like a conventional non-profit. Every day, I'm trying to figure out how to distribute leadership among my small team – composed of individuals with a wide range of relevant skills who are experts in their discipline – in ways that allow us to move forward with deep alignment and help us learn from one another to improve all our efforts.

While you might not be organizing within a formalized structure like we do, these questions are still relevant to developing your team. Division of labor is a necessary consequence of engaging in struggle online: you may need people who think about product and user experience, people who write code, people who produce still and moving images to complement your work, people with the facilitation skills to manage community, people who think about operational security online and addressing threats to the group, or people with any number of a broad host of other skills. There won't be any one person who has all of them – it's simply impossible to grapple with the complexity on your own.

To engage in transdisciplinary strategy is to engage in principled struggle across expertise. Being able to consider form and content at the same time – and understand how they are constantly shaping each other – is critical to being effective on the internet. At our best, our team operates from a deep trust of one another and our people, and at a speed where we are constantly sharing and challenging one another to expand our understanding of everything from movement dynamics to tech tools.

While we can't all master one another's skills, we *can* share a political analysis of the tools of our respective trades. That analysis can inform both how we show up for each other and what we ask of each other in our day-to-day work. It helps us see the intersections of our expertise and develop an interdependent way of looking at the work that makes every move intentional and considered. Our members respect us for this discipline.

Question Three:
What do we want people to feel, and how do our principles inform the politics of those feelings?

Some theorists of the economy of the internet have argued that the web is an economy of attention – with such a dizzying profusion of content, the thing that comes at a premium is attention. This turns the logic of the era of broadcast media on its head in a way that has broad implications for issues of censorship and speech online. In such an information-saturated environment, how do people make decisions about what they pay attention to?

I like to tell my team that people choose what to pay attention to based on how content makes them feel – what's the overall *affect,* or emotional content, of your offering? Affect is deeply political: the way we understand ourselves and our groups informs how we respond emotionally to news, analysis, and calls to action. It is also mutually constitutive. How we feel about the world around us impacts how we understand our identity in relationship with others.

Understanding that affect can be manipulated, and *manipulative,* is key to differentiating your work *as organizing*. Organizing helps people understand the things they're already feeling. At 18MR, we already know many of the folks who trust us for insight and analysis are used to feeling a particular way about the world. Helping them locate themselves and feel what it feels like to be in right relationship with the world around them is the work of creating belonging.

4 Question Four:
How does our work engage in placemaking online?

We approach all of the content that we put out, regardless of platform, as a body of work. It's not just about putting together a communications plan for a campaign or project, but rather projecting a sense of place through a combination of aesthetics, analysis, and effective action. It's not about the content itself so much as it's about an approach to the content — we create opportunities for our members to see themselves reflected in our work: their aspirations, values, and visions for the world as it should be, not just as it is.

Placemaking offline originates in city design philosophy that is oriented towards humans instead of catering to motor vehicle traffic or commerce. Principled placemaking is rooted in the ways that local communities already use the spaces in which they live and is informed by input from broad swaths of that community. It also isn't a one-time process, but rather iterative in response to evolving needs.

Therefore, placemaking online needs to be similarly oriented toward human beings. The results of successful placemaking on the internet are reflected in our members' willingness to give us candid feedback, the kinds of rich conversations that happen on our social media posts, and the sense of belonging we foster among our members. Additionally, because the content we create can, and does, get ported across platforms and reposted by other accounts, it's important that people can immediately identify it as coming from us, no matter where it shows up. Online placemaking is about a critical combination of writing style and design elements with principles, strategy, and affect.

5 Question Five:
How do we envision our collective efficacy?

All of these things combined together don't necessarily mean you're building power. The fifth and final question is exactly about power: when we think about what we do with all the work we put into the first four questions, the fifth asks, to what end?

Strategies that focus only on the community itself fail to contend for power in any meaningful way. While the relationships that are built and the analysis that is developed is critical to success, it is collective action that will keep people coming back for more.

I should also warn that rigorously answering the first four questions should protect you from drifting toward prioritizing the technology itself over the goals of your organizing. Insulating your thinking against the fetishization of particular tools is critical to building a sense of collective efficacy. And an engaged, disciplined membership will also mean you'll get pushback against campaigns where the form and the analysis don't align.

What I usually call the "given form" of online organizing will be familiar to most people: the petition and email, often with a thoughtful social media or content strategy thrown in on top. This approach is primarily focused on mass mobilization – deft writers might be able to politicize new folks around an issue this way, but it's more likely that you're turning out support from people who have already been activated around the issue in the past. The form is useful when you're trying to convince a target with power to act in ways that benefit your community or prevent harm. However, the form doesn't *necessarily* lead to building power.

> **We are intentionally and rigorously interfacing with some of the most insidious parts of surveillance capitalism.**

At 18MR, we think of our collective efficacy in more than one way. First, we do acknowledge the way mass mobilization tactics serve many of our goals. We keep these tools in our toolbox for this reason, and they're clearly legible to members. However, we also know that there is work to do that doesn't involve asking a legislative body to pass or repeal a law or a judge to grant a stay on a deportation order, for instance. Especially through principled collaboration with other movement organizations that specialize in other forms of organizing, we're able to model action that is expansive and generative.

Exploring – and sometimes developing – new tools for our people to see and experience collective efficacy online pushes us toward new forms. I'm particularly interested in finding forms that emphasize depth over breadth and create space for personal as well as social transformation. I'm interested in a much more nuanced field of practice that is also about how we build the future world in our everyday relationships, as well.

Building the Internet for Movements, Not Brands

You may have noticed that these five questions are deeply intertwined. I don't think that they're questions you answer once and then proceed to develop campaigns. They're meant to be a guide to an iterative process of asking difficult questions about what you're doing online, how, why, and for whom. Engaging uncritically with technology means having our work dictated by the constraints of that technology.

In order to contend for power online, we are intentionally and rigorously interfacing with some of the most insidious parts of surveillance capitalism. As we do so, we're trying to adjust the expectation for what organizing can look like online. A movement organization is more than a brand: brands are produced for consumption, but a movement is space for participation and power.

To abandon the internet as a site of struggle is not just to give into corporate power, as they work to enclose the online commons. It's also to concede a vast and undefined territory to the far right – cults of conspiracy, white supremacy, and violent nationalisms that run rampant even in seemingly mainstream online spaces.

We live in a time of tremendous opportunity for online action. Beyond the work that we have already done at 18MR, there's a constantly expanding horizon for what we *could* do. For instance, the possibilities for new kinds of international solidarities in a time of increasing authoritarianism and state repression are underexplored. The global pandemic also means more people are seeking belonging online, which is an opportunity and a threat.

The internet itself will not yield transformation and greater freedom unless we act on it strategically and in alignment with our values. It's my hope that this offering can be of use as we contend for power on the internet, using the internet. ⓐ

Cayden Mak is Executive Director at 18 Million Rising, a national organizing formation for young Asian Americans online. He is a movement technologist whose work focuses on making technology work for the people, while fighting coercive, extractive, and carceral technologies. He is the 2019 recipient of the Everett C. Parker Award for his work on media justice and internet freedom. He lives in Oakland, California.

Notes

1 Shoshana Zuboff, *The Age of Surveillance Capitalism: The Fight for the Future at the New Frontier of Power* (London Profile Books, 2019).

THE POWER OF SOLIDARITY AND MUTUAL AID: DECOLONIZING PUERTO RICO

BY PEDRO ANGLADA CORDERO

In memoriam Matilde Rodríguez Pérez (1934-2020)

Qe los cuentos de la abuela
de "en aqeyos tiempos de ante"
son los tiempos de aqí alante
disfrasaos con ropa nueba.
–Joserramón Melendes[1]

Marcelino and the Never-ending Work Shift

IN 1918, TOBACCO REPRESENTED THE SECOND MOST IMPORTANT EXPORT of Puerto Rico after sugar cane. Its production continued expanding until imported cigarettes took over during the 1930s, causing a devastating decline in the Island's tobacco production[2]. By the mid 1940s, my great-grandfather, Marcelino Rodríguez, was a living fossil of the colonial Puerto Rican economy. Due to his birthplace and social upbringing, Marcelino had learned every single step of the tobacco economy, from the agricultural phase to its production and the curation of the crop. By default, his children learned the trade from an early age, as well. Marcelino was not a land or farm owner. His family belonged to the socioeconomic class of the *agregados* – that is, the bottom echelon in the workforce hierarchy who lived on a plantation as part of the remnants of the nineteenth century Spanish economy of African slavery, followed by notebook labor and wage labor[3]. It did not matter that the government's land reforms of the time granted Marcelino a *parcela,* or land plot[4], to build a small home for his children. This was not an indicator of significant progress, nor did it bring financial stability. Success was far away for any member of the working class.

Regularly, Marcelino boarded the now disappeared train from Barceloneta to San Juan during a time in which both locations were so distant, Borikén seemed to be three times its size. As a middleman in the tobacco economy, he spent the week in Barrio Obrero selling his product. There was no romance in Marcelino's travels. The melody of *Lamento Borincano*[5] did not occupy his mind. Marcelino's reality kept him far from entertaining a popular song of the time. There was neither past in his memory nor future on the horizon, only a constant present. Marcelino's wife, Masimina Pérez, died young, leaving seven children behind to care for. Thus, Marcelino's most productive week at Barrio Obrero was not enough to meet the needs of his children. Neither was it enough to undo the family disruption that resulted from Masimina's death. From early on, the children had to join the workforce. My grandmother Matilde became a domestic servant at age eleven. She had to bring a younger sibling to live in the house that became both her work and domicile. The older siblings had to migrate to the tomato fields in Utah, the factories in Chicago, and Nuevayol.

The circumstances of Marcelino's life were parallel to the entire rural workforce in Puerto Rico. The 1940s are known to be a time of stark contradictions. The Island had hardly recovered from the social, political, and economic troubles of the 1930s[6,7,8], which brought the Island economy close to collapse[9]. With the beginning of World War II, all imports and exports of the Island were affected to such a degree that the danger of starvation was a possibility for the Boricua working class[10]. During this time, most programs funded by Roosevelt's New Deal, which were developed under the Puerto Rico Reconstruction Administration (PRRA) were on their way to failure. The Puerto Rico Glass Corporation and the Pulp and Paper Corporation, two of the most relevant industrial projects of the PRRA, are clear examples of how the oppressive dynamics of the colonialist policies of the United States, the hostility from capitalist private enterprises, and the colonial political opposition collided to sabotage government-run programs that could have brought some economic relief to a colonized country in crisis.[11] It

is not surprising that the demise of the economic relief programs of the time came from the same colonizing government body that funded it in the first place. Later work by economic historians reveal that the great majority of the funds spent in all of PRRA programs were funneled back into the United States economy[12].

The 1940s ended, and with them, the hopes of generations of workers who were impacted by the power of colonialism and all its forms of oppression. The first fifty years of United States rule proved to be a continuation of the interventionist practices that plagued the Puerto Rican people for 400 years under Spanish rule until 1898. The absentee white-collar brutality of the United States colonialism[13], the predatory power of capitalist corporations in the agricultural fields[14], the servitude of colonial political parties[15], and their mafia-like enterprises formed a *maraña*[16] of power dynamics that stymied Puerto Ricans in their ability to express and exercise their own will as a people.

The journey of struggle and suffering that Puerto Ricans endured for the first fifty-two years of United States occupation went on as if it never happened. All the abuses in the sugar cane fields, the political repression against pro-independence ideology, the sterilizing campaigns on women, these events that scarred Puerto Ricans for generations until present, were subjects that rarely made the headlines in the United States press. The American colonization brought an additional layer of isolation. Beyond the automatic isolation Puerto Rico is subject to due to its condition as an island in the eastern-most corner of the Caribbean, the island is also politically marginalized through its removal from the discourse that took place in the media from the beginning of the occupation. This isolation, perpetrated by the power of media and the ways in which history is documented, persists today in many forms, including language, the sanitization of historical facts, and other invisible barriers that result in acts of usurpation.

The acts of resistance against the power of United States colonialism of the 1950s through violence were a testament to the suffering that persisted for decades before. The promises of self-government of the time were not a reason for relief, but a reason for uprising in 1950[17]. For

Marcelino, and so many rural workers, life had continued without a day of rest, without time to reflect about the political turmoil around them.

The Real Taste of Piña Colada

ONE TYPICAL MORNING IN THE 1960s, MY UNCLE SATURNINO, A pineapple-field worker in Barceloneta, Puerto Rico, got up to go to work without knowing that he would never return home. Saturnino was not a pineapple-field worker by choice; his fate was predetermined by his place of birth, his parents' socioeconomic upbringing, their race. The relentless rain the night before had left the fields almost entirely flooded. Saturnino and his coworkers needed to work. The misfortune of their lives couldn't afford a day off. They insisted on working because the behaviors of the plantation owners were known to be voyeuristically inconsistent. They were laid off frequently for no real reason, and despite the unsafe circumstances of the field due to exposure to wet powerlines, it would not be the first time the crew worked under these unsafe conditions.

Saturnino was the first worker to enter the field in defiance of the *capataz*. Shortly after, his body lay dead by electrocution. Work resumed once the waters receded. Others took Saturnino's place in the field. His name was unimportant to the pineapple company. Then the pineapple economy that once scarred my family and the people of my barrio became insignificant in the capitalist agenda of the United States. When the pineapple economy collapsed, its demise was invisible to the colonizer. The fields were replaced with pharmaceutical companies, roads, funeral homes, and cemeteries.

The land reform projects that began during the New Deal era and that dragged on with the beginning of the new colonial government of the Commonwealth continued to bring more disappointments for years to come. The initial idea of the land reform consisted of *la tierra para el que la trabaje*[18,19]. This political platform was radical in nature. In essence, it represented the Zapatista principles. The new colonial leadership of the Commonwealth, while instrumental in persecuting and imprisoning people of pro-independence ideology, also understood the reasons why Pedro Albizu Campos was successful in gaining the trust of sugar cane workers to lead the strike of 1934[20]. As the leader of the Puerto Rican Nationalist Party, Albizu Campos dedicated his life to anti-colonialist pro-independence struggle through armed resistance. His success in leading the sugar cane strike, his incendiary rhetoric, and relentless political strategy made him the most dangerous figure against US imperialism in the Caribbean, for which he faced persecution, imprisonment and torture until his death in 1965[21,22]. Colonial politicians knew Albizu Campos was right in defining both colonialism and the working conditions of *la zafra*, slavery[23,24]. The colonial government could see the abuses of the sugar cane corporations through

their monopolies that dominated the Island. The land reform legislation attempted to break the sugar cane monopolies by redistributing and limiting the amount of land a corporation could possess[25]. The colonial government knew that if they could not improve the conditions of agricultural workers, squashing the political opposition would be meaningless, an uprising could happen again, regardless.

The colonial government's land reform initiative failed in its attempts at redistributing the land to make communities more self-sufficient. Nevertheless, it was partially successful in providing small land grants for working families to obtain property. This is how a lot of political loyalties were forged for generations to come. The sugar cane monopolies receded with the shift of the economy from agriculture to manufacturing. Corporations followed one key rule; if they were not controlling and exploiting the land, Puerto Ricans certainly could not either. The effects of this approach can still be felt in the present as Puerto Rico imports up to 85 percent of the food it consumes. With time, colonial governments hid their failure to include a sustainable agricultural plan in their economy by arguing that entertaining such a strategy represented a return to the past. Maintaining a negative perception towards agriculture on the Island was also effectively used for decades later as an axe against the independence movement. Today, Puerto Rico continues to feel the negative effects of capitalism perpetrated by the sugar cane monopolies that dominated the Island during the first fifty years after the United States invasion. United States Congress legislation from the distance has paved the way for the dysfunction of colonialism to continue pushing the Island into a dead end. Presently, the deaths of

On September 27, 1932, Hurricane San Ciprián struck the island.

workers like Saturnino repeat themselves in nurses dying in car accidents while commuting to three jobs that are not enough to sustain a family. The death of Saturnino occurs again in entire communities poisoned by toxic coal ash from highly polluted waste landfills. The death of Saturnino repeats again in generations of people who throughout their lives, worked, retired, and died in poverty because their pensions were taken by vulture hedge funds and the politicians that benefited from these corrupt schemes. Throughout time, the power of capitalism and colonialism under United States rule have proved to be toxic to Puerto Ricans. Those who have obtained power through colonial privilege have become another piece in the game of abuse and corruption. Much of what we thought we gained as people had been lost by the means of a power that insists in controlling our way forward. Solidarity among ourselves is all we have.

Hurricanes and Solidarity

The word hurricane comes from the Taíno word, *juracán*. To the Taínos, *juracán* was a god capable of manifesting nature's deadliest rage. For them, *juracán* was not specific to a powerful storm with intense winds. *Juracán* could have displayed its power through a severe drought, or perhaps an earthquake. This word became part of universal language the moment Europeans set foot in the Caribbean due to the high frequency of the storms. Hurricanes influenced the lives of the Taínos, and obviously, still influence the lives of Puerto Ricans and people of the Caribbean today. Hurricanes have the capacity to disrupt the normal routines of life. The destruction that comes with the rage of a hurricane is a rapid introduction to trauma. Psychologically, hurricanes make people aware of the realities they do not want to see or accept, including the deception of colonialism. Nothing can bring the people of the Caribbean to the remarkable collective awareness of endurance, resistance, survival, and solidarity like a hurricane. In fact, a hurricane in 1514 resulted in the first African uprising of the Americas[26]. Taínos and Africans came together in solidarity to form a new Puerto Rican identity fighting against slavery. A hurricane also initiated the collapse of the government in the summer of 2019.

Mutual aid work becomes essential for community functioning and survival after a hurricane.

The Manatí river cuts through my hometown, Barceloneta. The river flows about half a mile from my old family home, where I was *un chamaquito*[27]. When I first heard the high-pitch-screeching sound of the river like nails scraping metal, when I heard the snapping of trees being dragged by the stream in the middle of the night, I understood why the Taínos considered a hurricane like a god. After a big storm or a hurricane, my neighborhood and many others would always end up surrounded by water. Many others, under it.

I was about eight years old the first time I walked with my mother, my brother, and my grandmother into town after a storm to shovel mud out of my aunt's house, followed by her neighbor's. As I grew up, I repeated this same trip with my family carrying a shovel into town a number of times. After a hurricane or a big storm, actions like this one were very common in my community. One had to help with whatever was needed. Whether the work consisted in cutting tree branches, moving debris to open a road or a neighborhood street, or finding out where water, propane gas canisters, or other basic need items were available, mutual aid work becomes essential for community functioning and survival after a hurricane.

During the last several years, hurricanes and natural disasters alike have become notorious in exposing the corruption of colonialism, debunking false truths about dependency and the inability of communities to provide care for each other through mutual aid. During the aftermath of hurricane María, there were many narratives attempting to dominate the political discourse through the media. The narrative from the government of the United States attempted to minimize the impact of the storm by insisting that the aid provided by federal agencies was excellent. The colonial government tried to articulate that it had the situation under control. Both failed miserably. To this day, the two governments are unable to deal with the truth about the many deaths for which their neglect is responsible.

A narrative of powerlessness, of victimhood towards Puerto Ricans persisted for some time in the media after hurricane María. There is no denying that there was a humanitarian crisis on the Island. Hospitals were shut down. People were dying in them due to absence of treatment and care. Morgues were overflowing. Containers had to be brought in to store the bodies. The public paid for that. In many communities throughout the Island, there was no access to prescription medications, potable water, electricity, food, and other basic necessities. Despite these obstacles, it is undeniable that communities were doing the work of opening roads and making themselves accessible to receive and share aid when available. Both the colonial and federal governments failed in acknowledging the work communities facilitated for them. They continued to present a narrative of isolation and lack of access to justify their idle state.

Through the middle of the aftermath of the hurricane, several mutual aid initiatives emerged in different regions of the Island. These mutual aid efforts, sometimes known as *autogestión*[28], were ignited by many communities that were not in any way connected to the colonial government. All of them emerged organically without following specific political ideologies or theories. Still, their functioning based on collective solidarity while refusing hierarchical power schemes makes these organizations a model for how to decolonize from the root. The undeniable leadership of women, especially mothers and grandmothers, in these movements as agents of cultural change is essential in breaking old paradigms of oppression that mimic colonialist systems dominated by men.

Food and Crisis: The Great Unifiers

Not all mutual aid initiatives emerged as a function of a hurricane. For obvious reasons, however, hurricanes can produce the conditions of a crisis that would push communities to initiate sustainable mutual aid efforts. Food insecurity is probably the first sign of social stress that set communities in motion to provide care for each other in solidarity. The great majority of the mutual aid initiatives that emerged during the aftermath of hurricane María started providing food in impacted and isolated communities. This was the case of the *Centro de Apoyo Mutuo* in Caguas, *Mariana* in Humacao, *Bucamarones* in Las Marías, and *La Olla Común* in Río Piedras, among many others. Presently, all these organizations have evolved to diversify the services they provide to their communities. In the case of Caguas, the one project I had the opportunity to visit and support shortly after the hurricane, they started with serving food but moved on to rescue (occupy) a building, and today the project provides with limited shelter: a food bank; a health and wellness center that includes acupuncture; an urban garden;

workshops on earthquake preparedness, response, recovery and mitigation; and periodic people's assemblies, among other services. All other organizations have taken similar approaches involving art, theater, and other forms of progressive education strategies for children. All of the organizations have collaborated with each other in various community events and have embraced all Puerto Rican forms of cultures such as Bomba and Plena as a way of defining a new decolonized identity.

A different kind of crisis birthed a mutual aid-like organization that has become one of the most trusted community agencies in Puerto Rico. Casa Pueblo started in 1980 in the town of Adjuntas as a self-sustaining environmentalist organization. Casa Pueblo was formed to combat an open-sky mining proposal that would have destroyed the entire town of Adjuntas, and parts of Jayuya, Utuado, and other adjacent municipalities. The initiatives of Casa Pueblo brought a sense of unity and community leadership against environmental destruction. Later on, the organization took on the management of the Bosque del Pueblo, the forested area that would have been destroyed by the mining project. Bosque del Pueblo contains one of the remaining ceremonial sites of the Taínos. Casa Pueblo was never known as a mutual aid anarchistic organization, but as an *autogestión* project, one that evolved to serve the people. Its success provided a blueprint for many of the mutual aid efforts that surfaced after hurricane María.

Despedida

The practice of mutual aid in Puerto Rico and the Caribbean is an ancient tradition. Due to our place in the world as an island with subtropical weather conditions, by default, we are set to live in open communities. Our windows are always open. Everyone can hear what is going on in the neighborhood. There is a constant *entra y sale*[29] of people in communities. There is a constant exchange of goods among neighbors and nearby friends in communities. There is a constant flow of information about what is needed and where it is available in communities. You just put the word out there, and it makes it to where it needs to go.

I see my grandmother Matilde, at 86 years of age, putting mutual aid into practice. She turns the stove on, cooks some *guiso*[30], shares it with who needs it, and whatever she needs, whether it is a ride to a doctor's appointment, grocery store, or church, will be provided by someone eager to return the favor. It occurs organically, without political ideology or theory – just out of love and solidarity.

I return to the importance of mutual aid being initiated organically, with no political ideology or definition, because Puerto Rico is still finding the path towards its decolonization while it continues to be severely divided by political beliefs. Mutual aid initiatives on the Island have opened the doors of solidarity for communities outside of

political ideology. Therefore, there are people of all political spectra, from leftist pro-independence ideology to right wing pro-United States annexationists, to apolitical disenfranchised people actively engaged in mutual aid efforts, or at the very least, receiving and relying on their services. At first glance, these mutual aid efforts do not appear to be direct catalysts of decolonization, but they bring people with opposite ideas together to share a common purpose, to see a reality, one outside of the divisions and falsehoods that colonialism has imposed upon us for more than 500 years.

Coming together as people to initiate efforts that reinforce the sense of dignity and self-determination is an important step towards destroying colonialism. For those who are engaging in mutual aid but still believing in the colonial solutions imposed by our colonizers, they are one step closer to breaking with that illusion. Nevertheless, we are running out of time. The colonialist schemes of the United States government and their colonial politicians on the Island have led us into a dead end where time has been wasted into failure. Mutual aid efforts are strategies that can bring solutions to both short and long-term problems. They can help us to dismantle a dysfunctional government that operates by stealing money from the people and throwing change from the distance without focusing on problem-solving or long-term progress. History demonstrates that the main goal of colonial projects is to benefit the colonizer's economy. Mutual aid can be effective in helping us to finally walk away from colonial political party loyalties, which have caused the destruction of the Island. Mutual aid can help us finally understand that there will never be a better advocate for the Puerto Rican people than Boricuas themselves. This is what it means to decolonize. Ⓐ

---

*Born in 1976 in Río Piedras, Puerto Rico, **Pedro Anglada Cordero** is a writer and member of the resistance community in Portland, OR. His writing can be found at* Latino Rebels *and in* A Flash of Dark: An Afro-futurism Anthology.

Acknowledgements:

I dedicate this work to my grandmother, Matilde Rodríguez Pérez who passed away on July 10th, 2020. I would like to express my gratitude and love to her, and my mother, Madeline Cordero, for their lifetime support and family stories that are featured in this article. Thanks to my daughter Simone for all the love and laughter. Lastly, thanks to my wife Susan Anglada Bartley for all the love and camaraderie, the support with childcare and food, and for her criticism and editorial assistance before the submission of this piece. I love you!

Notes

1. Joserramón Melendes, *Desimos Désimas* (Río Piedras, P.R.: QeAse, 1994), 29–31.

   That the stories of the grandma / of "those times of the past"/ are the times here in present / disguised in new clothing. The author developed a writing style based on Puerto Rican phonetics where words are spelled to mimic the Puerto Rican collective voice. The poetry is meant to be sung or read aloud.

2. James L Dietz, *Economic History of Puerto Rico: Institutional Change and Capitalist Development* (Princeton, N.J.: Princeton University Press, 1986), 116–19.

3. Ibid., 40-52.

4. Ibid., 200-201.

5. "Lamento Borincano," Wikipedia, July 6, 2020, https://en.wikipedia.org/wiki/Lamento_Borincano.

6. Nelson A Denis, *War against All Puerto Ricans: Revolution and Terror in America's Colony* (New York: Bold Typed Books, 2015), 63–64, 116–20.

7. Pedro Aponte Vázquez, *Albizu: Su Persecución Por El FBI* (San Juan De P.R.: Publicaciones René, 2010), 5–60.

8. Dietz, *Economic History of Puerto Rico: Institutional Change and Capitalist Development*,160–177.

9. Ibid., 201-206.

10. Ibid., 201.

11. Ibid., 191-193.

12. Thomas G Mathews, *Puerto Rican Politics and the New Deal* (New York: Da Capo Press, 1976), 323.

13. Denis, *War against All Puerto Ricans: Revolution and Terror in America's Colony*, 44-52.

14. Dietz, *Economic History of Puerto Rico: Institutional Change and Capitalist Development*, 103-134.

15. Raymond Carr, *Puerto Rico: A Colonial Experiment* (New York: Random House, 1984), 107–36.

16. A tangled mess.

17. Pedro Aponte Vázquez, *Albizu: Su Persecución Por El FBI* (San Juan De P.R.: Publicaciones René, 2010), 89–183.

18. The land for those who work it.

19. James L Dietz, *Economic History of Puerto Rico: Institutional Change and Capitalist Development* (Princeton, N.J.: Princeton University Press, 1986), 193-201.

20. Nelson A Denis, *War against All Puerto Ricans: Revolution and Terror in America's Colony* (New York: Bold Typed Books, 2015), 109-131.

21. Ibid., 157-261.

22. Pedro Aponte Vázquez, *Albizu: Su Persecución Por El FBI* (San Juan De P.R.: Publicaciones René, 2010), 5-302.

23. Denis, *War against All Puerto Ricans: Revolution and Terror in America's Colony*, 109-131.

24. Ivonne Acosta, *La Palabra Como Delito: Los discursos por los que condenaron a Pedro Albizu Campos 1948-1950*, Editorial Cultural, 2000, 9-180.

Albizu Campos was sentenced to nearly 54 years in prison for delivering twelve speeches between 1948-1950. The speeches were documented by the police and used as evidence against Albizu. They were maintained sealed for 40 years until their release in 1991 as part of a Lawsuit filed by Pedro Aponte Vázquez. Acosta published the speeches that same year.

25. Dietz, *Economic History of Puerto Rico: Institutional Change and Capitalist Development* , 193-201.

26. J. Sued Badillo and Angel López Canto, "Puerto Rico Negro," *Editorial Cultural*, 1986, 175–185.

27. Youngster.

28. Self-initiative.

29. In and out.

30. Stew.

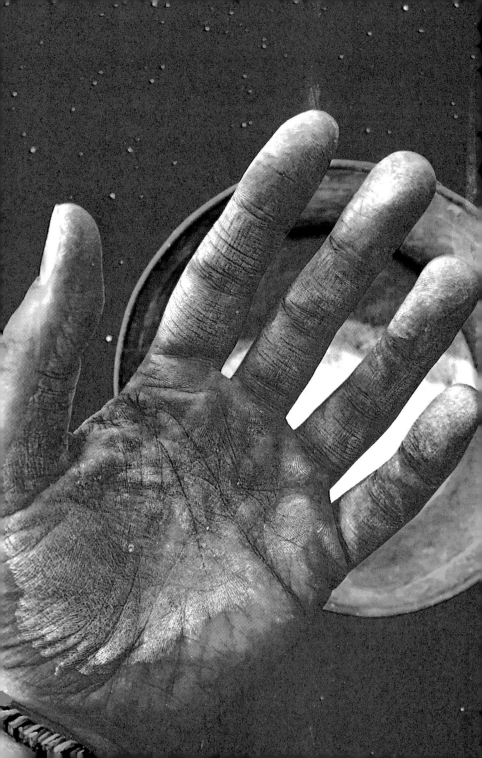

TIME UNDER TENSION
LESSONS IN ORGANIZING FROM A KETTLEBALL GYM

LARA MESSERSMITH-GLAVIN

Strength is a Skill

YOUR SPINE IS STRAIGHT. YOU HAVE SHIFTED YOUR WEIGHT BACK SO that your knees are above your ankles – this is such an uncomfortable position until you learn to trust the muscles that hold you there – and you check to make sure the bell is between your heels, not out in front of you. Your hands are slightly tacky with the chalk you've applied to absorb the sweat. The handle of the bell feels solid in your palms, its circumference just a touch wider than you'd like, the rough surface familiar to your grip. You turn on your lats by squeezing your shoulder blades together, and imagine you are cracking the handle of the kettlebell like a stick of kindling in order to activate your triceps. Do you feel equal pressure between your hands and your feet? You check, and then you initiate with the glutes to protect your lower back. The strain is immense at first, like you're trying to pick up a mountain, then you are pleased to find the weight glide smoothly upward as you stand in a perfect deadlift.

If you haven't lifted weights, you might be tempted to think that it's mostly a matter of brute force, that strength comes from muscle combined with determination and will. These things are important, but something kettlebell training has taught me is that strength is a skill. It comes from understanding systems and networks within the body and the brain; it comes from technique combined with practice and smart repetition, from knowing when to push, when to pull, when to tense or relax, when to breathe, and when to rest. It also comes from having a plan: strategic thinking, goal setting, and implementation over time with readjustments as necessary. These insights are more than just good lessons for creating changes in the body. In a lot of ways, they help me understand how to better create change in the world, as well.

It's not an exaggeration to say that kettlebells have saved my life. When I first started training, I was recovering from a life-threatening flare of an autoimmune disease; training brought back a positive relationship with my physical self and gave me a community in which to heal. Over time, I felt so committed to the transformative potential of the practice that I became a certified trainer at Bleeding Hearts

Kettlebell Club (BHKC) in Portland, Oregon, a city known once as "Little Beirut" and more recently as an "anarchist jurisdiction." Over the past four years, this gym has undergone a remarkable transformation of its own, resulting in a powerful site of activism and community support.

How have these changes happened? What makes a group of gym rats, weirdos, and housewives into a force for social justice? It's remarkable to me how much of what I see happening politically in our community genuinely seems to stem from our physical practice. What we learn in our bodies we can practice in community, and what we practice can grow into larger spheres of impact and change.

Stay Grounded

A common misconception with the strict press is thinking the arm or shoulder does the work. It's true that there must be an explosive burst at the beginning of a press to get the bell "out of the hole" and a slow burn to get it overhead, which does involve the triceps, deltoids, and traps, but to generate power, the key is to find your connection with the floor and press from the heel, developing an unbroken line of force from your root all the way to the bell. Many of us train barefoot so we can feel the floor beneath us and better control the angle of our ankles and hips, knowing that a key to strength is staying grounded.

Kettlebell training teaches that our base is the source of our power. If we have tension through the rest of the line but are unable to achieve a lift, we need to look to our base to make sure we are properly grounded, that the messages are traveling upward from the root. Just as this applies to the mechanics of a lift, we see the same principle underlying the networks that serve as the base of our organizing.

In the gym, this means staying connected to people and what their lives are about. Some folks are looking to reclaim their sense of self after a difficult period in their lives. Their goals may look different from those of people who have just given birth and are rediscovering their bodies in new ways. Others may be recovering from injury or committing to some kind of change in body composition, a personal goal, or supporting another sport or pursuit, while still others may just crave a healthy means of social connection. All of these are valid reasons to be engaged, and like any political configuration, there must be space for folks coming from all these different personal motivations for involvement.

It also means recognizing needs and barriers to engagement and making a concerted effort to lower those barriers. At BHKC, we provide inexpensive childcare, sliding scale membership costs and scholarships, alternative movements for different bodies' abilities, and an explicitly trans-, queer-, fat- and women-positive environment in an industry still dominated by cis-identities, thin bodies, and men's authority.

This doesn't mean the gym has always been a site of liberation. During the 2016 election, it was a hotspot of Hillary pantsuit liberals with deep investment in the electoral system, but the next four years showed the potential for change. What really made the eventual shift to radical praxis possible was starting in a place that made people feel welcome regardless of their fitness, their experience, their identity – especially for traditionally marginalized groups, or their personal motivations. We focused on helping them show up, making them feel like it was a place where they could belong, and then offering structural support (like childcare or a participation scale based on the concept of mutual aid) that would allow them to commit and stick around. The inclusivity was the starting point, not the ideology – or to be more precise, the inclusivity and structural support are fundamental components of the ideology. Making people feel welcome and meeting them where they are at is a political orientation that is too frequently skipped over in the pursuit of total alignment or perfection, which leaves our movement fractured, fringe-dwelling, and ineffective. We cannot control what brings people to the struggle. If we are patient and can start from a place of care that is genuinely unafraid of complexity, we are better able to form strong, diverse networks that will stay intact and dedicated through the long haul.

> **Kettlebell training teaches that our base is the source of our power.**

Consistency over Intensity: showing up

A common mistake that people make when they first get into any kind of fitness program is to dive in headfirst without a full understanding of their own capacity, work out intensively for a short period of time, and then either get injured, or get frustrated by a lack of immediate results and give up. These folks often walk away with a narrative of, "Oh, I tried [insert activity] once. It wasn't for me." But any true attempt at transformation isn't a quick taste – it's a commitment to a practice over time. A handful of ass-busting workouts will neither sculpt your abs nor enable you to pick up that big bell you see the slight woman across the gym handling with ease. What they will do is make you sore, and if you push too hard without also incorporating things like rest, sleep, and flexibility work that teaches about the ways in which your different physical systems are interrelated, you are more likely to see injury than gains.

The same goes for movement work. Sometimes, when a moment is hot and it seems like suddenly everyone is in the streets, folks will get activated and jump headfirst into the excitement that comes with times of rupture: the often liberating thrill of protests, the rich and beautiful swell that comes with first contact with expressions of solidarity, the sense of tremendous urgency, and of course the meetings after meetings after meetings. After throwing so much energy at a moment, it can seem impossible that change doesn't happen simply as a matter of course – we want it so badly! We're working so hard! The slowness of social transformation can feel glacial, unacceptable, untenable. Without taking care of ourselves – through rest, sleep, and flexibility work that teaches about the ways in which our different systems of oppression are interrelated, the ways in which history can offer both lessons and inspiration, and ways in which we have internal work to do, as well – it can be easy to burn out, get hurt, or lose the spark.

The metaphor of weight training is particularly useful, here: we are *training*. We are learning. It is a practice. One or two or ten big lifts is not what makes us strong. We train through repetition, building not just the muscle fibers needed to move increasingly heavy weights, but also developing the neural pathways, the timing, and the intuitions necessary for success. As we build muscle memory, we gain a sense of familiarity and trust. We know what our bodies can and cannot do, and where the fuzzy edge of potential between those lies. We know where the work needs to happen, and what we can rely on as foundations for the rest of our progress.

In organizing, it is also an ongoing practice that produces change over time. Our approaches may evolve as our needs and goals do. We may develop and try different strategies when circumstances shift. Most importantly, we maintain an ongoing presence in our networks and establish our reliability and familiarity. By showing up, we cultivate the fundamental trust necessary to do the difficult work that lies ahead.

For years, I was the token anarchist at the gym. It wasn't a secret, but it also wasn't exactly a selling point. It was just this weird quirk that one of the trainers had these ideas that lay outside the drumbeat of liberal activity and campaigns to wear pussy hats or get out the vote. I was also the person who programmed many of their workouts, taught them how to keep their bodies safe, and cheered them on whether they succeeded or failed. Our common pursuit was more important than the specifics of my convictions. Also, I was *their* anarchist, which meant that, when there were protests downtown and windows were broken, or when there were pictures on their social media feeds from the front lines of a standoff with riot cops, they felt safe in asking, "Why is this happening? Help me understand." And they trusted me enough to listen to my answers. Sometimes just maintaining that shared commitment and trust is enough to form a strong foundation of affinity. And with affinity comes the potential for action and change.

You Can Do Hard Things /
We Do More Work Together than Alone

Picture a timed carry or racked hold, with twenty people in the space, all shaking and straining in unison, sweat streaming down their faces and necks. Their muscles quake as they try to hold the tension consistent throughout their bodies, their shoulders and arms screaming to put down the weight. But they don't. The timer ticks on, time clearly slowing down in the moment, a minute lasting an eon. Some are holding more weight than they ever have before, having been encouraged or pushed or goaded by their coach or their friends. The load rides the line of unbearable, but no one breaks. When the buzzer goes off, there is a collective groan of relief as the bells are set down, some expletives, a few high fives.

We push each other to work harder and to resist the urge to give up when things are difficult. Then the moment passes, and we all find it's a little easier the next time around. We do far more work together than any of us would do alone. Plus, the experience of endurance is an important lesson in and of itself – to discover that we are capable of doing hard things and surviving, of succeeding. But doing so in community also develops our sense of togetherness and furthers a capacity for empathy that can extend into active solidarity.

At the gym, this has looked like noticing both the surplus of energy that is created through the collective bond and also harnessing it to do work in the world. Initially, as the community was still finding its political feet (the staunchly liberal years), this largely took the form of fundraising events for local charities, races and competitive workouts and costumed arm wrestling tournaments that both generated tremendous amounts of money for a range of groups, but also further solidified the sense of togetherness. The work toward a common purpose had a multiplying effect. At the peak of this stage, we raised $21,000 in one night for a queer youth resource organization, the result of both inspired generosity and months of dedicated work.

As a Trump presidency, the ascendancy of the Black Lives Matter movement, and dozens of other issues pushed people farther to the Left, the same sense of camaraderie developed emergent properties of motivation, momentum, and trust. An intersectional feminist book club developed as folks sought to educate themselves better and put their convictions into practice. Affinity groups formed, turning into street crews ready to roll downtown for protests. The lesson here is that when we team up, we are powerful – and this experience can happen where we are. We don't always have to go looking for sites to activate; there can be the potential for transformation in the places and communities of which we are already a part.

Everyone Cries on the Mat

Exercise stimulates neurotransmitter production, sometimes resulting in endorphin floods often described as a "runner's high." Sometimes the effort feels like a bonfire for pain, like it's burning off all the frustration, the anger, the sadness, transmuting negative emotions into positive work and bodily benefit. It is glorious, exhilarating, and freeing. Other times, it feels like it serves to pull you into your body rather than letting you float overhead in your brain. Rather than release, the effort merely wears away all the carefully constructed armor to reveal rawness and discomfort underneath. The same neurotransmitter activity that brings a high can open floodgates, as well, and sometimes the sweat on your face gets mixed with tears as something heavy is set free. Sometimes you don't even know why. When this happens, no one reacts other than to offer a high five or a quick, damp hug. Everyone cries on the mat.

This is another important lesson for us in our organizing spaces – creating space

We push each other to work harder and to resist the urge to give up when things are difficult.

for release and for loss. Under capitalism, everyone is wounded and hurting. Successful spaces need not only to offer inspiration and strategy for progress, but also to create space for pain and ways to process and heal. An aspect of becoming radicalized that I think is under-attended to is the grief that comes with it, for some. In my own process, as I learned more of history, more of the theory, more of the experiences of people who have the least to gain from our system, the more I had to let go of the sense of solidity that the framework offered and turn elsewhere for answers, models, and hope. Radicalization means divorcing oneself from dominant narratives and letting go of myths that are often so deeply held, they are mistaken for self-evident truths – like the idea that our productivity is a measure of our worth, or that cops keep us safe. This is obvious for some, but for others, stepping outside that story and imagining a new one is scary work, work which requires new and courageous forms of imagination. The truth is that the old story was always rotten, but letting go of even a rotten story can be frightening, as anyone who has done the difficult work of healing trauma can attest. As radicals, I think we can do a better job of helping people mourn their stories and former sources of pride, even as we encourage them to dream up better ones.

Cooperate, Don't Dominate

After doing a lot of shoulder work, you'd be smart to spend some time in what's known as an arm bar, resting partly on your side in a thoracic twist, with one arm overhead perpendicular to the floor, holding a light weight directly above the shoulder socket. It's not a lift, and it's not a stretch, exactly. It's a quiet moment of communication. It allows your nervous system to talk to your proprioceptive system and run a quick check to see how everything is going. Your shoulder muscles may twitch and dance as the larger muscle groups turn off and relax, and the tiny microstabilizers kick into action. After a few minutes, your shoulder will feel gooey and peaceful in a way that is difficult to describe, but that communicative work is key to joint flexibility, as well as to overall fitness and body learning.

Big muscles often get the attention – the biceps, the quads, the things people point out to admire when they've undergone hypertrophy after long periods of focused development. But health and strength require that all the tiny muscles are active and attended to, as well. If you've ever done a new or unusual exercise and woken up the next day sore in places you didn't know you had, then you understand how neglecting the little things can have big negative effects.

What this teaches us is that collaboration happens within the body as well as without. Different jobs require different actors, and all are important to the overall project. We need to pay as much attention to the small, interconnected bits as to the big, flashy pieces that get attention. Some folks are charismatic on the bullhorn and move masses with their words, but we also need the envelope stuffing, the soup making, and the everyday tiny efforts at inclusion and welcoming that hold the big movements together. It's the unnoticed labor that often keeps us balanced and moving forward, and for our organizations and efforts to thrive, we need to develop this balance with intention. If you are a leader personality, work on expressing gratitude and appreciation for the less prestigious work of others. If you are accustomed to operating quietly behind the scenes, know that you are essential and valued. All roles are important, and communication is essential to cooperative success.

All Systems Are Interconnected

Often a particular movement can be used as a diagnostic tool. As a trainer, I may ask a client who is struggling with their swing to show me their deadlift, instead, or one who is failing a press to demonstrate a clean. This is because movements do not happen in isolation, and habits of form that develop in response to one load or set of challenges can influence the way one approaches or handles others. A deadlift will tell me how someone is hinging and placing their weight, whether they are using their glutes or transferring the load to their quads or lower back. A clean will show me how one prepares for a press, what their rack position looks like and how they ready their body for tension. All systems are interconnected.

This is especially apparent to anyone who has ever been badly injured while training, myself included. Injury is often the result of an error in approach – overtraining, poor form, or compensation for weakness elsewhere in the system is revealed when something breaks down. It is common for folks to want to focus on the lifts they do well and under-develop those practices that are difficult or have less prestige attached – a big press is impressive, but nobody gets badass points for developing their plank endurance or being consistent in stretching their hip flexors. This often leads to imbalance.

For a long time, I swung very heavy with high repetitions; my musculature was plenty strong to manage the load, but over time, this practice revealed weaknesses and bone degeneration in my spinal column that were beyond my control or ability to heal, and I ended up with a catastrophic disc herniation that paralyzed my left leg. Recovery was incredibly slow and is ongoing to this day, but it also provided me with the opportunity to examine much more deeply how all the systems in my body are related and to strengthen them more equally, with an eye toward longevity over prestige. I had to put away the big bell and do things like precision core development and relearning how to balance, neither of which will get me marked any longer as the strongest guy at the gym. It forced me into a position of humility that was tough to swallow but has made me a more effective athlete and trainer in the long run.

This lesson is particularly difficult to learn in organizing work. Where are we overtraining, either out of habit or a longing for political capital or prestige? What are our weakest links? How can we continue to celebrate and employ our strengths while attending to a better balance of practices, including those we find the most difficult or the least likely to be rewarded with praise?

As the gym developed into a true community center, it was easy for it to be lauded as a model: an all-women staff coaching hardstyle kettlebells and Animal Flow, a large proportion of clientele identifying as queer or trans, a successful sliding scale model with scholarships available, childcare that was practically free. Yet even as we patted ourselves on the back for the things we were doing really well, there was a glaring problem that we hadn't figured out how to address – it was a community center, yes, but that community was largely white. We hadn't done enough to examine our own practices, our outreach, or the ways in which we were or weren't supporting the work and projects of our local communities of color, and it showed in the demographics of our clientele and training staff. Sure, part of the issue was geography – the gym is located in a neighborhood that is predominantly white, but that is true of many areas of Portland, and there were plenty of clients who traveled across town to train with us. None of them, however, were Black. We were attending protests, putting up signs, and engaging in tough conversations with one another and with others through social media, but we weren't doing the deeper work of listening and adjusting our model to make it genuinely welcoming and inclusive for a broader section of population. It was a serious weakness. It was time to look much harder at our practices and approach.

Get Eyes On

Sometimes what is happening in our own bodies may be more easily seen and understood from the outside. This is another potential lesson in humility – even trainers need to be coached. If one of us is struggling to break past a plateau in gains or is experiencing consistent pain that might indicate a problem in form, we have to be willing to swallow our pride and accept help from others, despite being "certified." We call this "getting eyes on" – asking for other trainers to watch our movements and get some perspective on where the errors may lie. It may only take a moment for another set of eyes to notice what is invisible to ourselves over thousands of repetitions.

The lesson here is that sometimes you need to ask for help. There is a secondary lesson inside of this, which is: ask first. Only seek help from those who are willing, and don't expect people to coach you for free. In other words, we weren't going to march up to our clients of color and demand that they help us make our space more welcoming to others. Instead, we sought out trainings and models that were available for us to educate ourselves better on how to transform our practices, to understand our roles in holding up white supremacy, and how to make lasting changes and commit to them inside and outside the gym. One aspect involved supporting trainers of color to establish themselves as leaders in the fitness community. We developed a fellowship program designed to provide access to practice and certification for athletes of color. Other aspects included doing the difficult self-reflective work of unpacking our own individual engagement in the movement and seeing clearly how we were failing to show up for Black-led organizing efforts on their own terms. This work is ongoing, and something we are committed to struggling with, in our work, our training, our personal lives, and our organizing.

Exhale with the Exertion

Gyms are traditionally pretty gendered spaces. Part of our work as trainers is to destroy this tradition and many of the expectations that come with it, and to help our community reprogram their notions of strength and of self. This often looks like helping people who have been socialized not to express power or ferocity to find it in themselves and tap it at the source. If you've been to an old-school iron gym, you know there's often a lot of macho grunting that goes on, something that you'll rarely hear in a workout space that is dominated by femme-identified folks. At the same time, not all of those noises are pure posturing – there are mechanical reasons behind certain shouts and explosive exhales, designed to generate power, tension, and the proper timing of exertion. One of my favorite breakthroughs with newer clients is when they learn to shed their shyness or the social programming that tells them to be quiet and not to take up space, and they learn to grunt to initiate force, particularly on a heavy squat.

Gyms are traditionally pretty gendered spaces. Part of our work as trainers is to destroy this tradition and many of the expectations that come with it.

The exhale is also key to the press and more complicated series of movements, like the Turkish Get-up. We practice what's referred to as "breathing behind the shield," holding tension in the abdomen while allowing our breath to move and act as a slow release of pressure, or in sharp bursts when needed. With more ballistic kettlebell movements, like the swing or the snatch, the breath is used explosively, and timing the inhale and exhale is key to both generating power and endurance. The disciplined intake of oxygen feeds the fire we are stoking in our cells. We learn to breathe so that we can keep going.

This lesson is simple: breathe through the hard times. Know when to push and when to relax. Breathe into the belly and use that breath to maintain focus and calm under stress. This applies whether we are in the streets or caring for children, writing or cooking or setting up phone trees, painting signs or doing jail support. This is true whether we are alone or working with a group. Breathe deeply, and exhale with the exertion.

When businesses began to close in March of 2020 due to the rapid spread of COVID-19, our gym closed its doors, as well. What we thought would be a quick shutdown to "flatten the curve" turned into a six-month hiatus in which all of our training and classes went online, with occasional, informal, distanced meetups in parks. The camaraderie that was so pronounced in person became abstracted and more difficult to maintain through screens, but we adapted quickly, lending out our bells to our clientele so they could continue training with us, modifying workouts so that things could be done in living rooms and backyards with minimal equipment, and offering individual check-ins so that people could maintain good form without the direct contact of in-person training. We used social media to stay connected with everyone, and the community responded in kind, sharing survival tips, mask templates, leaving treats and messages on doorsteps. We practiced mutual aid as if by instinct.

But as I write this, the pandemic wears on, and the numbers in the classes have dwindled. What makes us strong is a kind of presence, an experience that happens between us as physical beings in a physical space, and holding on to that is difficult as our time apart grows longer than any of us dared imagine at the beginning.

When in-person classes reopened on a very limited basis in September of 2020, the irony of working out in masks was not lost on anyone. After years of coaching people to be more explosive with their exhales, we now had to ask folks to do so with the most robust face covering they could manage; another kind of breathing-behind-the-shield. Our primary focus is on keeping everyone healthy and safe: our class sizes are strictly limited so that everyone has plenty of space; masks are worn continuously; there is no touching allowed in the gym, no more high fives – as the sign on the wall says, "Love people with your eyes;" equipment is not shared, and everything is bleached and mopped after every class. Many people still choose to work out from home, and we still offer prerecorded options and live classes through Zoom, trying to hold our community together. We continue to breathe – these are hard times.

Stay Fast and Loose

Sometimes when people finish a set, they look like they've only barely survived the experience. They lean over on their knees, panting, or sit down, or even lie on the floor. As tempting as collapse may be, it neither gives the body what it needs in terms of oxygen nor helps it recover for the next round. What we encourage folks to do, instead, is to bounce around lightly, to wiggle the arms and hands, maybe dance a bit if the music is right. We call this "staying fast and loose," which means keeping our muscles in motion without tension to improve blood flow and reduce stiffness. Even when we want to lie down, the best thing to do is just keep moving.

The bright side of the pandemic closure was watching the community blossom into other emergent forms and take positive action to help one another and to engage with the broader political moment. Affinity groups formed as members of the gym joined the thousands meeting downtown night after night to demand an end to police violence and to stand in solidarity with Black leadership. To support this work, the gym began pooling its experience and resources the best ways it could, offering free trainings via Zoom: basic protest safety courses, herbal aftercare for chemical weapons exposure, self-defense, Know Your Rights trainings. The space was shared with other political organizations, serving as a community hub. Food drives were organized, and members began engaging in jail support for folks arrested in the protests.

Affinity groups formed as members of the gym joined the thousands meeting downtown night after night to demand an end to police violence and to stand in solidarity with Black leadership.

What starts as an investment in community has the potential to grow outward if we let it. While we cannot anticipate all the ways in which circumstance and differences of opinion may influence the evolution of a group, by committing to one another and allowing what we are capable of doing to evolve, we can respond to the needs of the moment. The same is true for the tactics we employ – just as we have seen essential protest gear metamorphose from signs to reinforced banners to gas masks, an organization needs to be nimble enough to change its strategy as conditions develop. Instead of stiffening up, collapsing, or investing in a single form, we need to be willing to stay fast and loose, to allow ourselves to stay in motion so that we can be ready for whatever comes next.

Time Under Tension

There are no shortcuts to strength. If you want to get stronger, you have to put in the time under tension. The gains come from the long haul, not the individual sets. What coaching and training at BHKC has helped me understand most clearly is the power that comes from seeing revolutionary potential everywhere, even in the most unlikely of places, like a kettlebell gym. I believe in creating a coordinated program of transformation across society, but I think that also means we need to learn to organize where we are, to build things from the places where we live and work, to form the trust and networks with the people we see every day. We need to build things from the ground up in a way that allows for complexity and inclusivity rather than remaining marginal or maintaining a sense of purity or political perfectionism.

I believe that all sites of connection hold the potential for change. By investing in our communities, we can lead by example, even as we listen and learn from others. The commitment is to ourselves and to each other, to putting in the work. Bodies, needs, experiences, and even goals may be different, but a shared purpose can lead to tremendous capacity for change.

I know that in many ways, I am very lucky to work where I do. It helps that the owner of the gym has been undergoing her own journey of radicalization and is a tireless model of supporting her community. It helps that all the other trainers have the courage to do this work, as well, to interrogate their own complicity in white supremacy, to put their bodies on the line during protests, to stay connected to the community with both technology and endless amounts of spirit. Not all workplaces will shift in the way that my gym has – but at the same time, it isn't

a magical process, either. It's the result of patience, strategy, creating access to information, and genuine love. By developing networks of care, building trust, and offering or supporting leadership in hard times, we create models for all to step up. And as anyone who has worked out with us knows, we are stronger together. Ⓐ

Special thanks to Tana, Eloise, Lacey, Felecia, (and Rachel!), the other trainers at BHKC. I love you.

Lara Messersmith-Glavin *is a writer, teacher, and kettlebell coach in Portland, Oregon. Her work has appeared in numerous journals, zines, and anthologies, including* Still Point Arts Quarterly, Stoneboat Literary Journal, Radiant Voices: 21 Feminist Essays for Rising Up, *and elsewhere. Her new book,* Spirit Things, *is due out from the University of Alaska Press sometime in 2021-2022, pandemic depending. She is on the board of the IAS, and when she's not in a classroom or working on a book, she can be found performing onstage around the Pacific Northwest, exploring the woods with her child, or swinging bells at Bleeding Hearts Kettlebell Club. Check out her work at queenofpirates.net.*

FUNDRAISING ANARCHY

LAKE (CHELSEA) ROBERTS

"Put in very blunt terms, they had taken power – not by simply changing the names of existing oppressive institutions but by literally destroying those old institutions and creating radically new ones... Social revolutionaries, far from removing the problem of power from their field of vision, must address the problem of how to give power a concrete and emancipatory institutional form."

Murray Bookchin, "Anarchism and Power in the Spanish Revolution," *The Next Revolution: Popular Assemblies & the Promise of Direct Democracy* (Verso Press, 2015)

I AM AN ANARCHIST WHO WORKS AT A NON-PROFIT PUBLIC RADIO station. Yes, *that* public radio. A space that welcomes those among us who imagine a better world. If you've ever wondered where "Support for NPR" comes from, it's me. I'm a fundraiser. And of the many questions posed by the "Power Issue" of *Perspectives,* the one I return to almost daily is, "Is what we're doing working?" Unfortunately, for non-profit fundraisers, it's not.

It is no secret that the non-profit sector is mired in the same growth ideology that feeds capitalism. No matter what kind of non-profit fundraising work you do, you are likely familiar with our gleaming annual reports displaying infographics that prove the success of new initiatives, or you've no doubt attended "relationship-building" dinners that result in renamed programs honoring your biggest donors (or better, a responsible corporation). You understand how it feels to actually beam with pride at our organizations as they grow- grow- GROW. We mostly like our bosses. As fundraisers, we are people with visions, and needs like rent, so we can't help but throw ourselves into our work.

But after work, in a quiet moment, we hear what taps at the back of our brains and the center of our hearts. Something is wrong. As Bookchin states, liberating society is not accomplished only by building the good, but *by literally destroying* institutions of power to make way for radically new ones.

The people I know, I work with, and I really like, are highly skilled at building up and really bad at tearing down. Myself included. It's hard to admit that something isn't working, let alone attempt to dismantle a faulty system. But the non-profit industry's ideological assumption, our over-emphasis on growth, success, and positivity, is resulting in workplaces where we're unwilling to throw anything away, and then we wonder why nothing sparks joy.

Breaking Down

I have anarchist politics, which I broadly define as removing domination from society and interpersonal relationships to create an egalitarian, sharing society. The theories I subscribe to posit that domination can be removed on a two-fold path (or with a one-two punch if you prefer) of consciousness-raising and direct action.

I was pretty miserable at the start of my first fundraising job, and that isn't rare. Turnover rates are high in our line of work. If you are just getting started, rest assured that "making it rain" in this industry doesn't mean throwing cash, it's more like kneeling under the sky and praying. I stayed for the mission and the healthcare and the ability to set my own schedule. A year in, I got a few donors and started learning new things. It turns out rich people can be nice, and I hadn't known that. I had never been to lunch with a CEO or a person with wealth. My donors were funny and kind, and some really believed they were doing everything they could to help.

I thought I had cracked a code, "Could it be that rich people *just don't know?*" And if they knew, I mean if they *knew*, wouldn't they voluntarily redistribute even more of their wealth? What is stopping them from becoming my neighbor in this two-bedroom apartment complex next to the freeway? I have access now, I thought. I can change their minds. I can participate in consciousness-raising.

I began to dream of some kind of organization funded by the rich that lobbies for tax reforms to redistribute their own wealth. I thought I might be able to do that now with my increased access to people with capital. I know what you're thinking, no one with wealth would ever donate to something like that, but people make decisions against their own self-interest all the time. We sacrifice to live in community, albeit some more than others. I thought, seriously, there must be a few billionaires that would contribute to the "Bill to Tax Billionaires!" There are already conferences dedicated to providing a safe space for young people with wealth to investigate (and perhaps accept) their roles as "Changemakers."[1] I can't imagine the pun is *not* intended.

I thought, why can't there be anyone in the one percent who wants to truly topple the system? And how can I find them? As fundraisers we're always asking ourselves, "Who gets it? Who believes in my cause?" We are wrong when we think that simply finding more people who believe in education, ending hunger, journalism, and curing cancer, is the answer to our funding problem. Maybe we should be asking, "Who doesn't get it?"

In my first-year-fundraising schemes, the illness that is hoarding massive amounts of wealth stems from miscommunication, as though the data just hasn't been presented in the right way. For example, studies showing that happiness does not increase past an individual yearly income of $95,000 (adjusted and estimated for cost of living) prove there is no personal, measurable, emotional benefit to staying rich.[2] *If billionaires only knew*, I thought. That's it, they must not know![3]

But the thing is that they do know, ya know? I used to think like this because I am a person with anarchist politics: a person who chooses happiness, who wants to be filled with joy and help create that with other people. Influenced by my first-time access to people with extra capital, I dreamt that I could convince individuals to give away wealth in a series of decisions framed around their own happiness, which just happened to benefit the survival of the planet, and the dignity of humanity, because I was learning about philanthropy, and isn't that what it's all about?

> **We are wrong when we think that simply finding more people who believe in education, ending hunger, journalism, and curing cancer, is the answer to our funding problem.**

Unfortunately, no. Philanthropy is not about happiness. This is not the "Happiness" issue of *Perspectives*. Money will always be about power, even when we have enough. And yet serious discussions in our organizations about how we hold the line for the rich are dismissed, or worse, we tell ourselves it's an off-topic and irrelevant item for this meeting.

Our organizations operate like the private sector's funhouse mirror. While we are staffed with social-justice personalities and passion, we are entrenched in the second punch of social change, a constant rebuild. We work to create the radically new on top of dysfunctional systems that no one is willing to obliterate. And apart from the programs we deliver, which can be liberatory (I care about journalism,) the way most of us are funding our programs does not contribute to the better world we know is possible. This is the non-profit industrial complex, in 2021.

But First, It Gets Worse!

In Anand Giriharadas' book, *Winners Take All: The Elite Charade of Changing the World* (Knopf, 2018) he criticizes non-profit-*seeming* "think tanks" led by "thought leaders," which prize "innovation" (my actual trigger word) and enlightened corporate self-interest as the solution to the problems facing our planet.

Giriharadas states, "All around us, the winners in our highly inequitable status quo declare themselves partisans of change. ... They may join or support movements initiated by ordinary people looking to fix aspects of the society. ... More often, though, these elites start initiatives of their own…these initiatives mostly aren't democratic, nor do they reflect collective problem-solving or universal solutions."[4]

For example, last year, Salesforce CEO Marc Benioff spent $30 million funding a research institute associated with the University of California at San Francisco which promises to "research causes of homelessness."[5] As Julianne Tveten argues, the many causes of homeless are known. Regardless of research, what she calls "capitalist charity" will not solve them. Also last year, Jeff Bezos built a homeless shelter in an Amazon office building in Seattle. Cool. Regardless of the PR blowout and ribbon-cutting, these "helping" initiatives do not actually solve problems: they showcase power, using misdirection with help from some press to balance growing complaints about the way Salesforce and Amazon's business practices displace people from San Francisco and Seattle, respectively.[6]

Corporations find no irony in funding causes adjacent to the problems that their very existence exacerbates.

These corporations find no irony in funding causes adjacent to the problems that their very existence exacerbates. They are not afraid of blame, critique, or retaliation in the form of regulation. And why should they be? As long as they work towards "solutions" that do not compromise their own wealth, championing what is good while ignoring dissent, they're doing what is expected of them.

In contrast, the San Francisco poor-person led coalition *POOR Magazine* has maintained a strong critique of capitalist philanthropy for years, defined as solutions administered with the express consent and direction of the wealthy.

From their website, "Philanthropy which has its roots in the Slave/Master 'plantation' model, operates from the premise that people with money and/or resources inherently hold more knowledge about money than people without money. Contrary, we believe that people who have struggled to survive, feed and clothe multiple family members and themselves in fact hold a deep scholarship about the use and distribution of resources."[7]

They operate on a yearly budget between $300,000- $600,000. They have only recently begun to receive some grant assistance and they have started a project called, "homefulness," a poor person-led solution to the gentrification crisis plaguing San Francisco. Imagine what they could do with $30 million.

As non-profit workers, although we are not always representative of the communities we serve, we don't have to operate like solution-designers either. We can research the poor-person led, Black and Indigenous

People of Color (BIPOC)-led, youth-led movements and organizations that inspire us. We cannot let our visions be co-opted by large corporations that cover their most embarrassing problems with cash.

Consensus-based small programs that change lives are currently operating in the squatted basements of buildings, rented by despotic economic philosopher kings – who pay out five percent of corporate foundation earnings in absence of tax to the cities they operate in. This kind of corporate "giving" will never challenge capitalism, but it will crowd out non-profit programs. How many people know about *POOR Magazine*? How many people know about Salesforce?

When The Revolution Will Not Be Funded

Foundations exist to fund non-profits, provided there is a good fit. Foundation funding priorities are not surprising: education, homelessness, medicine, the environment. A private, corporate, or family foundation typically chooses cause areas and geographic locations, then distributes funds annually through grant competitions.

Foundations fall short of the "Bookchin test," (which I'm making up right now), because of the way they reward reformist, as opposed to revolutionary action. Foundations have a reputation for not funding the first punch. They want their money to have a good impact, they want pictures, usually, charts and graphs, and other metrics of success. Many foundations prefer to fund programs that can "demonstrate measurable impact." It's difficult to get grants for things like journalism, for example. How do you demonstrate the measurable impact of truth-telling? Of an informed public?

In my experience, foundations prefer to fund school lunches and send corporate t-shirts for kids to wear at summer camps. They may say that their funding impacts social change, but what direction are we heading in? Is the current funding system working to address social concerns like poverty, homelessness, lack of access to education, food, medical care, and information? Is what we're doing working?

For radical organizations it is even more difficult, "reliance on foundation and/or government funding adversely impacts the course of community mobilizing and organizing."[8] Anne Petermann, founder of the Global Justice Ecology Project states, "Even when liberal foundations appear willing to fund grassroots organizations and movements for social change, [often] their true intent is to push for the types of limited reforms that address various social problems in a manner that does not challenge the prevailing power structure of American capitalism. As a result, liberal grantmaking tends to dilute, rather than support, radical protest."[9]

Participating with foundations makes radical organizations vulnerable to co-option, pressure, censorship, lack of stability, and a volatile market. INCITE!, a grassroots network of radical feminists of color, discovered this in 2004 when their $100,000 Ford Foundation grant renewal was declined because of the group's political statement in support of Palestinian liberation. This is an example of a foundation's overt control over a non-profit, but how many of us self-censor, even at the time of writing a grant request? When Petermann states that liberal grantmaking dilutes radicalism, she is not describing a one-way street.

Foundations generate investment income from the stock market so, broadly speaking, what is good for capitalism is good for them. Foundations are required to grant out a certain portion of their earnings (usually five percent), or they are subject to taxes. During times of crisis, foundations are often called to spend out more than five percent, but there is no legal requirement. And during difficult economic times they still must spend the five percent. An average market should earn about seven percent per year, so if the market does poorly the foundation will "go out of business." Those wealthy people would have to pay taxes, and they wouldn't get to pay out five percent of their investment incomes to causes they choose. Why then would foundations fund something disruptive to capitalism?

There are a few alternative grantmaking models, and some may be more interesting to anarchists. At first glance an organization like the Washington Women's Foundation might seem less culpable in capitalist ideology because they call their model "collective giving." By convening women of some means who can contribute $2,000 per year (instead of say, five million), they make philanthropy accessible to the middle class while donating $500,000 per year in grants to local organizations.

The Ralph C. Wilson Foundation in Detroit operates by "spending down," meaning they intentionally give more money than they earn with the intention of closing the foundation. To "spend down" is kind of radical. Rather than build something that is designed to grow and maintain power (and paperwork) for generations to come, these foundations distribute the power (money) they have into the community regardless of market outcomes. And when the foundation closes its power has not expired, but has flowed freely into the community where it is now wielded by others. Spend down mandates might come from a wealthy founder, or be implemented as a response to the pressing nature of social problems.

The End

Ultimately, funding non-profits keeps lunches in school, kids in summer camps, medical researchers in the lab, public radio on the airwaves, immigrants nearly out of cages, and more. It solves the many, many problems of our world by building positive experiences and attempting to right wrongs.

But rarely are non-profits able to poison capitalism at the root by diverting money towards tax legislation, lawsuits, protests, and massive, collaborative direct actions against, *against!* specific, predatory businesses and powerful individuals. What might that look like? Would you apply for that job? We must insist on flipping the coin between dismantle-create, destroy-rebuild, so we can directly transform our era, as Giriharadas states, "in which capitalism has no ideological opponent of similar stature and influence." We have to come clear, and sometimes that means being a downer.

Why do I do this? Wouldn't I be happier in a job that knows it's a job, without all the deep compromises and loud rhetoric of social justice? I'm not sure. Capitalist growth ideology tells us to chase solutions, but anarchism tells me to take a look at what is in front of me and that means contradictions. Rich people are actually generous, kind of. They do want to help! Sort of.

I am solving problems, I think. Things are changing, maybe for the better.

Foundations generate investment income from the stock market so, broadly speaking, what is good for capitalism is good for them.

Fundraisers understand these contradictions. We meet every day with people who say they want to solve problems, give back, and make a difference. But at the end of the day, they don't want it badly enough. If they did, they'd give up the power it would take, and to hell with the money. They'd give it all away and that generosity would shock the system. They'd put me out of a job. And I'd have to give up being such a critic.

Here are five ways I get out of bed:

One. I stay focused on what I've learned: Real, transformative action is more possible (and more exciting) outside of philanthropic giving. We are not getting paid to tear down the system. If you want to tear down the system, there are many ways to do that, probably contained in the rest of this issue.

Two. Money is the means to the end of the work my organization does. I love *that* work, and make space for myself in it. I love public radio. I read our articles, I champion our reporters. When I waited tables I always made sure to work somewhere I wanted to eat every day.

Three. We're not trapped raising money (unless you count living in capitalism). Fundraisers have many skills like writing, empathy, patience, persistence, and more technical skills related to finance. We're here because we want to be here, as complicated as it is. We've chosen to participate.

Four. To the point that I am able, I am sincere about my doubts and frustrations at work. I suggest actions. This doesn't always go over well. I volunteer my time as a grants consultant for BIPOC-led orgs.

Five. I strive to protect myself from implicit growth ideology. My side hustle is writing, and so I read books, surround myself with people, media, and messages that check me. That inspire me. I try to leave work at work. I am real about the way participating in institutional giving compromises my politics. I live between a radical "scene" and a more or less normal life. I assume I'll look back on my working years and remember the words of Muriel Rukeyser, "Most days, I was more or less insane."

Is what we're doing working? Not really. We're not tearing down existing institutions of wealth and power because, as non-profit workers, we rely on them to survive. Ⓐ

Lake (Chelsea) Roberts is a writer and artist from Michigan. Her research into the Living Theatre was published this year in the Journal for the Study of Radicalism *(Michigan State University Press). Her play critiquing gender-based hierarchy in higher education, "the masters," has been workshopped in Seattle. More at www.ChelseaLakeRoberts.com*

Notes

1 "Making Money Make Change 2019," Resource Generation, accessed January 23, 2020. https://resourcegeneration.org/events/making-money-make-change/

2 Andrew Jebb, Louis Tay, Ed Diener, and Shigehiro Oishi, "Happiness, income satiation and turning points around the world," *Nature Human Behavior,* 2, 33-38 (2018) https://doi.org/10.1038/s41562-017-0277-0

3 We would've done well during our non-profit training (if we got any!) to read Anne Petermann, founder of the Global Justice Ecology Project, who bleakly states,

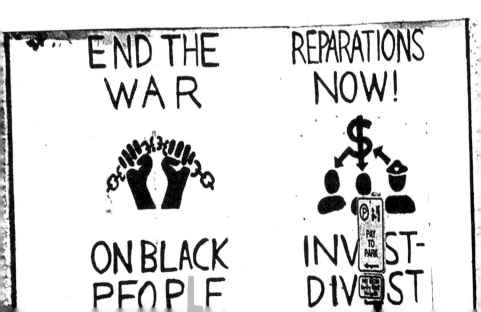

"Rather than challenging state power, the nonprofit model actually encourages activists to negotiate, even collaborate with the state." https://www.socialpolicy.org/spring-2012/528-fundraising-politics-and-strategies.html

4 Anand Giriharadas, *Winners Take All: The Elite Charade of Changing the World* (Alfred Knopf, 2018), 5.

5 Julianne Tveten, "Capitalist charity can't solve homelessness or any other social problem," People's World, accessed Jan 23, 2020. https://www.peoplesworld.org/article/capitalist-charity-cant-solve-homelessness-or-any-other-social-problem/

6 Big Tech Isn't the Problem With Homelessness. It's All of Us," Wired, accessed July 27, 2020. https://www.wired.com/story/big-tech-isnt-the-problem-with-homelessness-its-all-of-us/. and "Photos show how big tech is turning Seattle into 'San Francisco North,'" Business Insider, accessed July 27, 2020. https://www.businessinsider.com/seattle-amazon-microsoft-tech-boom-photos-2019-2. and "Picking Up The Pieces: Five Ways The Tech Industry Can Help Fix The Homeless Crisis," Forbes, accessed July 27, 2020. https://www.forbes.com/sites/forbestechcouncil/2019/08/27/picking-up-the-pieces-five-ways-the-tech-industry-can-help-fix-the-homeless-crisis/#253562a93787. and "MORALES AND SAWANT REINTRODUCE LEGISLATION TO TAX AMAZON," South Seattle Emerald, accessed July 27, 2020. https://southseattleemerald.com/2020/03/05/morales-and-sawant-reintroduce-legislation-to-tax-amazon/.

7 "Become a Revolutionary Donor," Poor Magazine, accessed July 27, 2020. https://www.poormagazine.org/rev_donor

8 Luz Rodriguez, review of *The Revolution Will Not Be Funded: Beyond the Non-Profit Industrial Complex,* by INCITE! WOMEN OF COLOR AGAINST VIOLENCE, *Philanthropy News Digest,* December 20, 2007. https://philanthropynewsdigest.org/off-the-shelf/the-revolution-will-not-be-funded

9 Anne Petermann, "Fundraising: Politics and Strategies," *Social Policy*, accessed January 23, 2020. https://www.socialpolicy.org/spring-2012/528-fundraising-politics-and-strategies.html

CHRISTOPHER FRANCISCO (DINÉ)

ECONOMIC JUSTICE

POLITICAL POWER

FOR ALL PEOPLE

COMMUNITY CONTROL

DAVID GRAEBER
Feb. 12, 1961 - Sept. 2, 2020

DAVID GRAEBER &
THE POWER OF IMAGINATION

JAMES ANDERSON

DAVID GRAEBER DIED IN EARLY SEPTEMBER 2020. HE WAS 59.
In an essay he authored, titled "Dead Zones of the Imagination: An Essay on Structural Stupidity," anarchist geographer David Graeber started with an anecdote about wrestling with the medical bureaucracy to assist his mother who had suffered several strokes.[1] She died soon after, he revealed a few pages later.[2]

That someone whose work was so influential in shaping my own ideas about the world and how to change it is now gone, and that I can nevertheless still read what he wrote broaching the subject of death, strikes me as significant. The assumed significance compelled me to dig deeper into that essay once again while contemplating the arguments he articulated in that piece in relation to the profound insights scattered throughout so much of his work.[3]

Returning to his writing and immersing myself in it after his death revealed just how applicable much of it is to the current conjuncture. Amid the novel coronavirus pandemic made a million times worse by global capitalism and its institutions, coupled with righteous indignation and insurrectionary mobilizations against racist police violence, Graeber's words still resonate, perhaps now more than ever. But in lieu of eulogizing, which others have already done so beautifully, this commemoration will proceed by way of engagement with the powerful ideas Graeber shared through his accessible, public-facing work. I draw heavily from his critique of bureaucracy and structural violence.

I also work with a theme developed throughout his work – imagination. As Graeber acknowledged, "the word 'imagination' can mean so many different things."[4] In popular parlance today, it is often conceptualized in the abstract and "counterposed to reality; 'imaginary' things are first and foremost things that aren't really there."[5] However, Graeber also made clear just how practical and indispensable imagination is in the formation of human lives worth living and in the reproduction of social relations that make our lives meaningful. Taking it further still, he alerted us to the ways society impairs the human imagination, redirecting it toward pathological aims in the service of bureaucratic systems intent on imposing unrealistic expectations bound to a simultaneously violent and stupid order. I hope to show how the power of Graeber's imagination can still ignite our own creative capacities capable of catalyzing struggles and constructing strategies geared toward transcending a wrong world rife with hierarchical violence and stupidity.

Markets and Capitalism: Beneficiaries of Bureaucracy and Agents of Structural Violence

Let us begin with bureaucracy. Be it metaphorical piles of electronic paperwork, an explosion in administrative and managerial occupations, or the oft-labyrinthine systems of rules imposed by those with claims to the legitimate monopoly on violence that govern ever-greater facets of our lives, bureaucracy is having a moment. Graeber claimed we had entered an epoch of "total bureaucratization."[6]

We can also interpret the political spectrum in relation to people's positions vis-à-vis bureaucracy. Insofar as one subscribes to the notion, dating back to around the time of the French Revolution, that the political spectrum can be divided into a left-wing and right-wing, "the Left, in its essence," Graeber wrote, "is a critique of bureaucracy, even if it's one that has, again and again, been forced to accommodate itself in practice to the very bureaucratic structures and mindset it originally arose to oppose."[7] He went on to suggest that the lack of a potent critique of bureaucracy from the Left in the last four or five decades is synonymous with the lack of a potent Left in recent years.[8] Failure to advance a vision beyond the bureaucratic morass that has enveloped the body politic weakened the Left and spayed liberatory, anti-authoritarian movements whose raison d'être had long been about abolishing bureaucracy in the process of birthing something new.

We can hardly separate the failure from the duplicitous celebration of markets, those institutions so deceptively yet inextricably linked to the ascendancy of bureaucracy. Graeber put forward a sociological theory he called "the iron law of liberalism," which "states that any market reform, any government initiative intended to reduce red tape and promote market forces will have the ultimate effect of increasing the total number of regulations, the total amount of paperwork, and the total number of bureaucrats the government employs."[9] Although it is not the only economic system or form of socioeconomic organization to do so, capitalism clearly tolerates and even brings about – perhaps increasingly requires – bureaucratic institutions.

This becomes all the more evident when we factor in another one of Graeber's arguments. The argument focuses on "structural violence," by which he meant the "forms of pervasive social inequality that are ultimately backed up by the threat of physical harm."[10] He elsewhere defined it as those existing "social hierarchies backed up by a systematic threat of force."[11] Whichever way you slice it, Graeber argued that structural violence produces disparities in "interpretive labor"[12] and in capacities for "imaginative identification"[13] – disparities that in turn engender a form of social stupidity managed by bureaucracy. Social arrangements of structural violence are inherently stupid insofar as they generate "lopsided structures of the imagination," owing to the fact those empowered by the stratified arrangements do not have to engage in the interpretive work typically necessary for the maintenance of human social relations. Those ultimately able to exercise, or to enlist a repressive apparatus in wielding, violence to maintain the conditions that benefit them (at the expense of others) need not empathize with the people systematically disempowered by those same conditions who, in contrast, must imagine what those in power want and need. Those subject to structural violence, and/or to the direct physical violence Graeber stressed as the foundation for the former, regularly work to interpret the world from the perspective of those positioned to tell them what to do. The subordinate and subaltern are obliged to empathize and envisage the world from the point of view of persons in power, lest they bear the brunt of that impending violence or suffer injurious injunctions on agency worse than the constraints on consequential human thought and action ordinarily operating in structurally violent spaces.

The connection between direct physical violence and structural violence is also of the utmost importance here. As Graeber once wrote,

> Violence is veritably unique among forms of action because it is pretty much the only way one can have relatively predictable effects on others' actions without understanding anything about them. In any other way one might wish to influence others, one has to at least know or figure out who they think they are, what they want, find objectionable, etc. Hit them over the head hard enough, it all becomes irrelevant.[14]

Graeber made clear just how practical and indispensable imagination is in the formation of human lives worth living.

He added that relations of violence have historically characterized interactions among different societies.[15] Violence simplifies social relations. When we humans have lacked complex knowledge about each other, we have resorted to such simplifications.

Interestingly, as Graeber also documented, barter (or market exchange more generally), has seldom if ever emerged from within a given society; rather, it tends to "take place between strangers, even enemies."[16] Drawing upon the tradition of world-systems analysis, Graeber elsewhere pointed out how many now believe capitalism "developed first in long-distance trading" before it "gradually wormed its way into ever-more-intimate aspects of communities' daily life."[17] Commercial exchange cropped up to simplify social relations among parties without the requisite knowledge or affective inclination to interact in the complex ways traditionally enabled by community life.

> **Violence simplifies social relations. When we humans have lacked complex knowledge about each other, we have resorted to such simplifications.**

Both violence and the market transactions required for capitalism, then, serve a similar function in terms of minimizing the importance, at least for some, of interpretive-imaginative labor. "Most human relations – particularly ongoing ones, such as those between longstanding friends or longstanding enemies – are," Graeber maintained, "extremely complicated, endlessly dense with experience and meaning. They require a continual and often subtle work of interpretation; everyone involved must put constant energy into imagining the other's point of view."[18] Violence and market exchange privilege formulaic ways of interacting by eschewing and impeding the richness of social life. Graeber noted that this is why "violence is so often the preferred weapon of the stupid,"[19] and we could add that markets, like bureaucracy, have become one of the preferred mechanisms for managing systemic stupidity.

Of course, markets – even without the wage labor and class antagonism central to capitalism – can also aggravate existing disparities and give rise to situations of structural violence. Market abolitionists like Michael Albert, a proponent of "Participatory Economics"[20] whom Graeber credited with "an important achievement" for working "out a detailed plan for how a modern economy could run without money on a democratic, participatory basis,"[21] have often pointed this out.[22] Per Albert's critique, while humans have different abilities to benefit and produce for each other, who can produce more or benefit others better – or market themselves, if you will, to give people that impression anyway – can demand and obtain more through market systems, though those differing abilities should not automatically bestow a moral claim for select persons to benefit more. In a similar vein, markets permit those with greater innate abilities to reap better economic rewards even if they exert less effort or make less sacrifice on the job, thereby rewarding or disadvantaging people for what can be outside their control while not truly incentivizing or properly valuing approaches to labor we can control. Furthermore, markets reward those with greater ability to hold out and wait to reach an agreement. This puts a strong, healthy and able-bodied person without dependents at an advantage over, say, a single mother with a sick child, to borrow a common example. Markets also advantage those with greater or easier access to certain goods and materials, making mere proximity to desired resources and essentially happenstance a determining factor in who gets the best deal. Finally, the wealth conferred by those who exercise the most power within market systems in turn confers social power that extends beyond the institutions for allocating goods and services through competitive buying and selling. Concentrated social power then reinforces the structural violence resulting from the hierarchies erected by the market exchanges giving rise to that social power to begin with.

To be sure, markets are necessary for, but they are not unique to, capitalism. As Graeber pointed out, one can say capitalism exists "when profit becomes an end in itself" and capital incessantly endeavors to expand.[23] As he also noted, one can define it based on wage labor and claim it "occurs when a significant number of firms are owned or managed by people who hire others to do their bidding in exchange for a direct payment of money, but otherwise have no stake in the enterprise."[24] However, Graeber argued, we can also view the advent of capitalism as coeval with the systematic separation of the economic from the domestic sphere – a split that makes abstract talk of the "economy" possible.[25]

Abolitionist and Feminist Insights Regarding Police and Bureaucracy

But back to bureaucracy and violence, both of which have recently thrived under capitalism. Policing, the subject of much debate as of late, buttresses both. Graeber connected the market ideology integral to capitalism with violence and the police, and he wrote,

> Whenever someone starts talking about the "free market," it's a good idea to look around for the man with the gun. He's never far away. Free-market liberalism of the nineteenth century corresponded with the invention of the modern police and private detective agencies, and gradually, with the notion that those police had at least ultimate jurisdiction over virtually every aspect of urban

life, from the regulation of street peddlers to noise levels at private parties, or even to the resolution of bitter fights with crazy uncles or college roommates.[26]

He went on to lament how we have become so used to the notion that we *could* (and lots of people, I'd add, still believe we *should*) call the police to resolve just about any problem that "many of us find it difficult to even imagine what people would have done before this was possible."[27] Yet, as Graeber emphasized, for most people throughout human history, there were no authorities to call in such situations – "at least, no impersonal bureaucratic ones who were, like the modern police, empowered to impose arbitrary resolutions backed by the threat of force."[28] Yet we now take it for granted that police ought to intervene in circumstances they historically would have had no business intervening in, just as we have come to accept the bureaucratization of everyday life as legitimate. Graeber called cops "the immediate representatives of the state's monopoly on violence, those who step in to actively simplify situations"[29] when, for instance, somebody challenges the reduction of social life to some pre-conceived idea incapable of accounting for the ambiguities of existence. "Police," Graeber wanted to remind us, "are bureaucrats with weapons."[30]

His historical insights are in accord with many principles of prison-industrial complex (PIC) abolition, like the notion we have abdicated responsibility for each other by coming to rely on police to resolve myriad issues of social harm. Graeber also highlighted how our learned dependency on law enforcement became so naturalized. He pointed out that we do not usually think about policing as the enforcement of regulations, and instead assume police primarily fight violent crime. However, "what police mostly do is exactly the opposite: they bring the threat of force to bear on situations that would otherwise have nothing to do with it."[31] Obfuscation about that reality abounds, Graeber offered, because "in the popular culture of the last fifty years or so, police have become almost obsessive objects of imaginative identification,"[32] protgaonists of many a media narrative portrayed as protectors who keep us safe, not as defenders of private property with a knack for executing racist state violence.

Yet, Graeber went further. Thinking about the function of police (and bureaucracy), he wrote, allows us to look at social theory in new light. Both bureaucratic knowledge and theoretical knowledge involve radical simplifications and purposefully reductive generalizations; they frequently entail application of pre-existing paradigms. In the realm of theory, though, he insisted, "simplification is not necessarily a form of stupidity – it can be a form of intelligence,"[33] even a source of profound elucidation. "The problems arise," he added, "at the moment that violence is no longer metaphorical."[34] Then, himself moving from the abstract to the concrete,

David Graeber speaks at Maagdenhuis, Amsterdam, March 7, 2015.

he cited sociologist Jim Cooper, a former LAPD officer, who stated the one behavior guaranteed to provoke a violent police response has to do with people calling into question an officer's presumed right to "define the situation" and apply a preferred administrative template to maintain what passes for social order.[35] The corporate state's bureaucratic imperatives and its monopoly on coercion come together in a police officer's exercise of force. "It only makes sense then," Graeber clarified, "that bureaucratic violence should consist first and foremost of attacks on those who insist on alternative schemas or interpretations."[36]

In a brilliant rhetorical convergence, Graeber proceeded to illuminate the connections between police violence, bureaucracy and the imaginative-interpretive labor deficit driving the stupidity of a structurally violent – that is, a highly and illegitimately hierarchical – society. As Graeber explained, situations of structural violence ultimately remain in place because of a real threat – and indeed, the periodic deployment – of state-sanctioned brutality. Those situations also exist because bureaucracy helps conceal the undergirding reality while administering all of the rules and regulations that keep the state and capitalism afloat. These factors give rise to those uneven imaginative capacities. Within the part of the population that sits atop many social hierarchies, the underlying structures, buoyed by bureaucracy, stifle the innately human yet also learned abilities so crucial to the collaborative self-care and reproduction of our species.

Just as Graeber's argument echoes a philosophy of abolition – not surprising given his affinity for the anarchist tradition and the opposition to coercive state structures running through it – his criticisms also echo those leveled by feminists and abolition feminists in particular. This is also not surprising, given that Graeber explicitly credited feminist theory and Critical Race Theory with having already articulated many of the same ideas he espoused.[37] He foregrounded his feminist critique in his explanation of how structural violence places the burden of interpretive labor on subordinate persons while rendering it superfluous to those in dominant institutional roles. He referenced the way institutionalized power disparities running through gender relations have historically placed the onus on women to figure out what men want, while men have chalked up their inability to understand women to the supposed fact that women are so fundamentally different and presumably impenetrable. "For example," he wrote, "in American situation comedies of the 1950s, there was a constant staple: jokes (told, of course, by men), always represented women's logic as fundamentally alien and incomprehensible."[38] The popular message on those shows would be something along the lines of the following: "You have to love them, but who can really understand how these creatures think?"[39] In my mind, one can accept that genetically endowed biological differences influence socio-culturally manifest iniquities pertaining to sex and gender while still acknowledging and working to overcome the historically constructed patriarchal residues that influence sexual politics and perpetuate institutionalized gendered hierarchies that subordinate women to men.

One of the primary reasons opting out of interpretive labor has not been an option for many women has to do with the powerful pillar propping up structural violence. If you recall, Graeber adamantly underscored how direct physical violence and the threat thereof create situations amenable to structural violence. Historically, patriarchal relations survived in part because of the direct physical violence men could use to threaten and to subjugate women, especially in the domestic sphere.

> **As Graeber recognized, exploitative structures warp the imagination in different ways depending upon the context.**

If you also recall, Graeber viewed the split between the economic or productive sphere and the sphere of domestic relations as a fundamental facet of capitalism. The split reinforced patriarchal gender norms. Like abolition feminists, Graeber grasped these intersections. In relation, he also understood how the work of producing people, which takes place primarily in the personal and domestic spheres, falls disproportionately on women. Capitalism, which privileges the production of commodities to be bought and sold on the market, devalues all the energy and effort that goes into making other people, it devalues the persons predominantly tasked with that work, and it devalues the non-economic spheres in which the extensive labor of tending to and cultivating other human beings unfolds.

Ironically, in the economic realm, employment of the imagination is not always asymmetrical. High-ranking executives or mid-level managers acting on behalf of a corporation might truly perform a decent amount of interpretive labor on occasion in order to encourage employee loyalty and commitment to a company's competitive success. The reverse can also occur, commensurate with the thesis explained above. Yet it would be a mistake to minimize the role of those that Albert, the aforementioned market abolitionist, refers to as "the coordinator class of managers, lawyers, accountants, engineers and others who are empowered by their positions and responsible for much daily decision-making and definition of workplace structure and activity."[40] Sometimes termed the "professional-managerial class" in political discourse,[41] this strata accounts for approximately a quarter of the workforce and monopolizes the empowering labor that allows for greater understanding on (and often off) the job. Existing class society and the corporate division of labor largely spare them from the rote, tedious and monotonous work those lower in the workplace pyramid end up shouldering, as their positions require taking orders coming down from on high. Individuals comprising the "coordinator class" have frequently benefited from the intergenerational transmission of social and cultural capital they could parlay into an elite education and coveted occupational status. That status then affords them a degree of affluence and comparatively greater leisure time. All of that tends to be more conducive to creativity which, like desire, Graeber considered a vehicle of the imagination.[42]

Yet, as Graeber recognized, exploitative structures warp the imagination in different ways depending upon the context.

> They might create situations where laborers are relegated to mind-numbing, boring, mechanical jobs and only a small elite is allowed to indulge in imaginative labor, leading to the feelings, on the part of the workers, that they are alienated from their own labor, that their very deeds belong to someone else. It might also create social situations where kings, politicians, celebrities or CEOs

prance about oblivious to almost everything around them while their wives, servants, staff, and handlers spend all their time engaged in the imaginative work of maintaining them in their fantasies. Most situations of inequality I suspect combine elements of both.[43]

Conditions of structural violence that characterize socioeconomic relations within capitalism can indeed induce feelings of alienation.[44] If you do not own or finance productive property, you have little choice but to sell your capacity to work for a wage. Doing so puts you in competition and at odds with others vying for the same position or for the same sort of industry work, alienating you from others in your socioeconomic class. One performs work for a company not to meet one's needs directly, of course, but in order to earn a wage, which alienates you from that labor. So too does your lack of control over how the work is done, since those doing the work are rarely afforded opportunity to partake in the decision-making processes that determine workplace tasks and conditions. As a Marxian critique would emphasize, you are also alienated from the surplus value you produce that the owners realize as profit on the market. A firm does not remunerate you for all of the contributions you make to the production of economic value for the enterprise because if that were the case it would make little sense to hire you.[45] Likewise, alienation can ensue because you do not own or control whatever you help produce or the services you provide, as those become commodities for market exchange. Commodification and the related, reductive market transactions mediate and estrange us from one another as well. The market's erasure of exploitative wage labor that furnishes commodities and helps create economic value – along with its effacing of all the labor that goes into producing people who can work for a wage – no doubt alienates us. The layers of bureaucracy inserted to administer situations of structural violence embedded in that matrix preserve alienation, and all that prevents the power of our imagination from unleashing a wave of institutional transformation.

Even as we recognize the various barriers to imagination fashioned by relations of subordination, then, we ineluctably return to Graeber's key insight regarding asymmetries in interpretive labor and imaginative identification. Graeber challenged the notion that knowledge is invariably tantamount to power when structures of violence are at work (note

Graeber challenged the notion that knowledge is invariably tantamount to power when structures of violence are at work.

the operative double entendre). Imaginative identification, viewed "as a form of knowledge,"[46] regularly gets short shrift among many employers who turn around and expect, unrealistically (not unlike the hierarchies and bureaucracies demanding obedience to rules with which humans can hardly comply), that workers tap into some psychic powers in order to appease the boss. Graeber summarized the situation as follows:

> Anyone who has ever worked in a restaurant kitchen, for example, knows that if something goes terribly wrong and an angry boss appears to size things up, he is unlikely to carry out a detailed investigation, or even to pay serious attention to the workers all scrambling to explain their version of what happened. He is much more likely to tell them all to shut up and arbitrarily impose a story that allows instant judgment … It's those who do not have the power to hire and fire who are left with the work of figuring out what actually did go wrong so as to make sure it doesn't happen again.[47]

The class conflict baked into capitalism at the enterprise level not only precludes the practice of economic democracy that could give working people greater say over the workplace decisions that affect them. It also precludes the democratization of imaginative identification within a structurally violent system.

Death, Domination, and Transcendence

Now, not to dwell on death, but Graeber provided another apropos example for feminist and anti-capitalist theory dealing with how we memorialize the departed. In fact, he argued, the phenomenon of mourning reveals some of the "essential labor of people-making"[48] insofar as it shows how much of one's social standing stems from the work of others. In line with what we have adduced so far, societal expectations have long ensured women disproportionately engage in the under-appreciated labor of mourning. Moreover, Graeber suggested that without much of the "labor of people-making" and the values that make social reproduction possible, there would be no real source of value in the economic sphere under capitalism because, as alluded to before, without that you would not have functioning individuals capable of selling their power to work for a wage.

Interestingly, while mourners' actions recreate the conceptual separation between the earthly and divine, as Graeber indicated, capitalist society, characterized by the split between the domestic/personal and economic spheres, also supposes a transcendent realm.[49] The economic arena – the space outside and apart from domesticity – "is usually treated as if it is to some degree transcendent, that is, as floating above and unaffected by the mundane details of human life (the special domain of women), having to do with timeless verities, eternal principles, absolute power – in a word, of something very like idealist abstractions."[50] Mourning, as described above, is another form of denigrated labor, performed overwhelmingly by women, "which creates and maintains that illusion of transcendence."[51]

The disconcerting myth of transcendence, however, appears to be more a product of capitalism's arrangements than it is a consequence of constantly co-creating human beings. Like capitalism, Graeber claimed, "all systems of domination seem to propose that," truly "there is some pure domain of law, or truth, or grace, or theory, or finance capital, that floats above it all," even as "such claims are, to use an appropriately earthy metaphor, bullshit."[52] The bullshit flies under our radar most of the time, as does the fact capitalism benefits from the value we place on our collective co-creation while the system simultaneously masks and demeans that creative people-producing process.

Effectively, our desires, passions, commitments and other human qualia entail "processes of the mutual creation of human beings,"[53] but economic value and associated idealist abstractions conceal our mutually constitutive processes by positing a higher sphere. The more hierarchical a society, the more that is the case.[54] As noted before, Graeber contended that the simplifications of social theory could be incredibly useful, but he also observed that historians, social scientists and, we could add, philosophers routinely engage in odd simplifications about human life and people's motivations that really miss the mark because of this presupposed transcendental realm.[55] The ideologies that emerge thus serve to reinforce values amenable to the constant accumulation of capital.

For his part, Graeber advanced one final thesis among several in a paper authored in the 2000s that captures the way capital, the engine driving the dastardly system, relies upon the reification of our otherwise emancipatory imagination. "Capitalism's unlimited demand for growth and profit," he adduced, "is related to the transcendent abstraction of the corporate form."[56] Extrapolating further, he went on to assert that the "dominant forms" within any society are treated as "transcendent forms," similar to the way we regard forms of value.[57] Troublingly, he added, "when these "transcendent forms encounter 'material' reality, their demands are absolute."[58] He did not expound upon that final claim in the essay. To my knowledge, he never had the chance to expound the claim at all. He left it for us to interpret. The best I can do is to connect the transcendent corporate forms under capitalism to relations of domination. Capitalism empowers corporations to act like what another anarchist-minded academic, Noam Chomsky, refers to as "largely unaccountable private tyrannies"[59]

Bureaucracies manage the stupidity stemming from dehumanizing social hierarchies by stupidly refusing to address the realities of lived human experience.

detached from any meaningful input workers directly subject to decisions in firms could offer and estranged from any significant influence the wider public impacted by business might wish to exert. We would be remiss not to similarly connect the totalizing or absolute demands made upon people by capitalist institutions and the virtually all-encompassing control exacted by bureaucracy in this era.

Coincidentally, though, Graeber's imagination, as expressed in the form of theory, ostensibly transcends the life of his human form, which left this world far too soon. Fittingly, the power of his imagination implores us to do the interpretive work and the imaginative identification he cited as so essential to who we are and to who we shape ourselves to become. Graeber's thought prompts us to consider what lies beyond the dominant transcendent imaginary with regard to the possibilities of human imagination.

The Hegemony of Bureaucratic Realism

In his essay on structural violence and bureaucracy that I have referenced throughout, Graeber quoted the famous slogan from the uprisings of 1968 – "Be realistic: demand the impossible."[60] Too often, being told to be "realistic," as he argued elsewhere, means being urged to acquiesce to and recognize the omnipresent, "systematic threat of violence,"[61] even if those issuing the imperative rarely state that explicitly. In arguing for recuperation of the radical – albeit practical – imagination and attendant praxis to realize what so many of us automatically dismiss out of hand as impossible, Graeber was careful to distinguish that from the utopian nature of bureaucratic systems. As he put it,

> Bureaucracies public and private appear – for whatever historical reasons – to be organized in such a way as to guarantee that a significant proportion of actors will not be able to perform the tasks as expected. It's in this sense that I've said one can fairly say that bureaucracies are utopian forms of organization.[62]

It is here that Graeber opens up the notion of what it means to be realistic. Bureaucracies manage the stupidity stemming from dehumanizing social hierarchies by stupidly refusing to address the realities of lived human experience. This transpires to the degree bureaucracies "set demands they insist are reasonable, and then, on discovering that they are not reasonable (since a significant number of people will always be unable to perform as expected), conclude that the problem is not with the demands themselves but with the individual inadequacy of each particular human being who fails to live up to them."[63]

Graeber does not make this point explicit, but we can also see how an ideology of individual responsibility might gain ground, given the bureaucratic structures erected in ways that make it impossible for people to abide. That ideology, like the bureaucracy it supports, appears to, as Graeber had it, "create a culture of complicity,"[64] a fealty to existing institutions. If Graeber is correct in stating that bureaucratic systems smack of utopianism "in the sense that they propose an abstract ideal that real human beings can never live up to,"[65] then those systems (of structural violence) hijacked the popular imagination to such an extent that an "era of total bureaucratization" could emerge. To flip the ideological script, we could say that the individualization of social problems derives from entrenched structural violence and from the bureaucracy that manages it while holding all of us up to unrealistic ideals; that logic succeeds insofar as we fail to assume responsibility for letting it seep into nearly every crevasse of social life. Likewise, capitalism's drive to produce, and to reduce human beings and other parts of the natural world to commodified things, and its separation of the domestic from the economic sphere, comports with a worldview that downplays the collective efforts directed at creating vibrant social creatures (human beings habituated to thrive).

Granted, like Graeber was at pains to show, the ideological serviceability and sustained influence of the above surely depends quite a lot on the state (and right-wing militia-style) violence waiting in the wings to pounce should direct action begin to seriously challenge prevailing institutions. For him, "the essence of right-wing thought," amounted to "a political ontology that through such subtle means [like the euphemism of 'force,' evocative of cosmic action, used in place of state-sanctioned harm] allows violence to define the very parameters of social existence and common sense."[66] Despite his skepticism of the present-day utility of the Gramscian concept of hegemony, referring to the cultural processes producing popular consent for a social order in ways that naturalize dominant organizational forms, Graeber remained privy to the ways human constructions, even and especially those at odds with real human flourishing, become normalized and legitimized. His writing about pop culture depictions of heroic police officers is Exhibit A. However, he also remained attentive to the real ways that coercion and repression reinforce the maintenance of hegemony. Future contributions to Gramscian theory might do well to investigate that and the interplay between bureaucracy and hegemony.

We have to raise the question here, though, as to how and why people come to consent to coercion and repression. Bureaucracy seems to help. It assists in the management of stupidity, thereby inculcating unjust idiocy. It also circumscribes and redirects the imagination, especially when would-be rebellions start intimating that our imagination might take material forms. Police and agents of the prison-industrial complex are adept at imposing shackles on people's imaginative powers, literally and figuratively. Graeber also understood that the bureaucratic and thus "profoundly alienating" institutions defining our existence "are the instruments through which the human imagination is smashed and shattered."[67]

Hegemonic images of heroic cops and the cultural construction of criminality come equipped with advertisements that help sell not only goods and services, but also the prevailing order.

Although it is beyond the scope of this essay, we at minimum must acknowledge how the dominant commercial media system, through which all those televisual shows stretching the limits of our ability to imaginatively identify with others via obsequious veneration of law enforcement, also amplify experiences of alienation. This seems similar to the way intrinsic features of structural violence affect interpersonal relations so that, according to Graeber, those most victimized by the system "tend to care about its beneficiaries, or at least, to care far more about them than those beneficiaries care about them." [68] In effect, "apart from the violence itself," that concentration of empathy and concern among the subjugated occupying lower rungs of hierarchies could, per Graeber, account for "the single most powerful force preserving such relations."[69] In like manner, hegemonic images of heroic cops and the cultural construction of criminality come equipped with advertisements that help sell not only goods and services, but also the prevailing order.[70] Televisual consumption comes replete with repeated exposure to ads that manufacture new wants, needs and desires by playing on our anxieties and insecurities.[71] After the drudgery of alienating work, we seek out entertainment to try to allay our condition, and in so doing we encounter ads that encourage us to buy products. Persuasive ads, like those designed to make us feel inadequate so long as we remain without the commodity for sale, drive us to work harder and harder

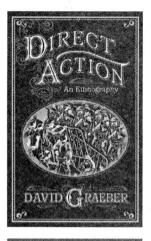

and longer and longer. We thus subject ourselves to greater and greater experiences of alienating work in order to obtain the wages needed to purchase what has also been produced by exploited, alienated labor. A vicious cycle ensues.

It all appears far worse if we factor in the new media environment. Corporate social media platforms commodify the user-generated content we openly share with others so they can sell that data to third-party clients who thereby collect the information needed to target us with eerily personalized ads.[72] We become "infinitely exploited,"[73] serving as the source of value and profit for companies like Facebook and Google without receiving any wages in return. In place of payment, tech companies offer access to the sites and apps that manipulate behavior and stimulate digital addictions (alongside depressive symptoms related to excessive social media use). Emergent experiences of alienation that result thus further reinforce the status quo in part by taking advantage of our dissatisfaction with it. All the while, our imagination is funneled into ad-induced fantasies about individual gain that come at the expense of action in common that could furnish more fulfilled human beings.

Insurrectionary Upheaval and the (Transcendent?) Power of the Radical, Practical Imagination

Notably, Graeber seized upon the idea that moments of insurrection "are moments when this bureaucratic apparatus is neutralized," and that has "the effect of throwing horizons of possibility wide open," as would be expected given the customary function of bureaucracy to "enforce extremely limited horizons."[74] Open rebellion opens up a realm of possibility on multiple fronts. Graeber noted that "just as during moments of revolution institutionalized structures of statecraft are dissolved into public assemblies and institutionalized structures of labor control melt into self-management, so do consumer markets give way to conviviality and collective celebration."[75]

Herein lies another part of the enduring relevance of Graeber's radical imagination. Prior to his premature departure from this world, he gifted us theoretical tools for discovering what potential resides in the uprisings of 2020 – uprisings that quite clearly reflect rebellions against structural violence. Most pertinently, contestation of structural violence has come in the form of widespread mobilization against the systemic racism and institutionalized anti-Blackness on display in the murder of people of color by the state-backed bureaucrats with guns. Secondly, the structural violence of a system that has rendered millions of people disposable during the COVID-19 pandemic, leaving large swaths of the population with no jobs, income or money to pay rent, contributed to an outpouring of support for militant demonstrations.

The perennial problem we must grapple with again has to do with how the insurrectionary activity of 2020 can contribute to thoroughgoing structural transformation.

The perennial problem we must grapple with again has to do with how the insurrectionary activity of 2020 can contribute to thoroughgoing structural transformation. As Graeber noted, the question posed by erstwhile revolutionaries had "thus been: how does one affect fundamental change in society without setting in train a process that will end with creation of some new, violent bureaucracy?"[76] As part of a partial rejoinder to his own rhetorical question, Graeber cited another '68 slogan, "All power to the imagination," but he promptly raised another germane question regarding what imagination we are referencing there.[77] On one hand, there is "the transcendent imagination" that leads to attempts "to impose some sort of prefab utopian vision"[78] as atrocities abound. Then there is "the other, immanent sort of imagination – the practical common sense imagination of ordinary cooks, nurses, mechanics and gardeners," which under the right circumstances might be vital if we are to avoid violent imposition of a bureaucratic schema under the guise of bettering humanity.[79]

As readers are likely aware, currents of insurrectionary – and, it is important to note, currents of reactionary and proto-fascist – thought operating during this period of interlocking crises believe a civil war in the US is fast approaching and, some contend, even desirable. In his work published a few years back, Graeber seemed far less sanguine about the prospects of anything good coming out of that mode of militarism. He referred to "the old assumption that a single uprising or successful civil war could, as it were, neutralize the entire apparatus of structural violence, at least within a particular national territory," as "strikingly naïve," given what we know about past insurgencies – even if it certainly appeared as though movements could nullify or control the apparatus during those revolutionary moments.[80]

One way to resolve the dilemma we face involves using our inbuilt abilities to imagine and interpret the world from a different perspective. (You should be noticing a theme, by now.) As Graeber noted, movements since the sixties have reframed the issue by lowering their sights.[81] Rather than think of it as lowering the bar, though, Graeber is getting at the frequent implementation "of the logic of direct action," which he defined as "the defiant insistence on acting if one is already free"[82] – effectively putting theory creatively into practice, albeit in ways that have heretofore left a brutal and impinging bureaucratic context intact. Following Graeber here, we can expound upon direct action as

> a form of action in which means and ends become, effectively, indistinguishable; a way of actively engaging with the world to bring about change, in which the form of the action – or at least, the organization of the action – is itself a model for the change one wishes to bring about. At its most basic, it reflects a very simple anarchist insight: that one cannot create a free society through military discipline, a democratic society by giving orders, or a happy one through joyless self-sacrifice. At its most elaborate, the structure of one's own act becomes a kind of micro-utopia, a concrete model for one's vision of a free society.[83]

Working under the assumption that, as Graeber had it, "anyone who takes part in a direct action is likely to be permanently transformed by the experience,"[84] anarchists often endeavor to embody a beacon of possibility able to attract and inspire others. To move beyond individual and ephemeral change, to displace bureaucracy and to regularize the principles of direct action, Graeber understood, engagement with other communities, even those looking askance at the unfolding of latent possibilities, and strategic engagement with surrounding authoritarian systems, becomes necessary.[85] The repressive carceral apparatus of the state, and the accompanying hegemonic culture extracting our tacit consent for the repression used to maintain capitalist society, adds a layer of difficulty to that engagement. With not only media texts and popular culture generating consent for domination, but with alienating bureaucracy blocking our ability to imagine and entertain other ways of being, the prospects for engaging in authentic ways look bleak.

How, then, can we keep the radical imagination alive while coalescing insurrectionary upheaval and everyday actions that cut against the grain into visions and strategies capable of winning a world without capitalism, the state or other co-opting modes of bureaucratic authority?

Well, if we are "to start in that direction," Graeber seemed to believe, "the first thing we need to do is to recognize that we do, in fact, win some."[86] As he documented, by way of the Global Justice Movement, the Left (opponents of bureaucratic violence more generally) managed a direct action-driven defeat of the worst of the World Trade Organization and International Monetary Fund agreements and policies. Before that, the anti-nuclear movements of the late 1970s and 1980s, while oftentimes unsuccessful in the short-term, won a near-moratorium on nuclear power plant construction and the legitimation of new forms of "feminist-inspired direct democracy"[87] in the process.

Like Graeber, we can also start thinking "of capitalism as a very bad way of organizing communism."[88] "Perhaps everyday forms of communism are really – as Kropotkin in his own way suggested in *Mutual Aid*,[89] even though … he was never willing to realize the full implications of what he was saying – the basis for most significant forms of human achievement, even those ordinarily attributed to capitalism," as Graeber explained.[90] Under many if not most circumstances, we "assume that the idea of each according to his or her abilities, to each according to his or her needs – in solving a problem – is actually the only thing that works."[91] That kind of communizing activity turns out to be "the basis of all sociality and it's the basis of cooperation,"[92] as demonstrated on the daily by friends, family members, neighbors, and co-workers. Our quotidian ways of relating to one another reflect low-key communism and anarchism. When disaster strikes, mutual aid often further displaces hierarchical and authoritarian systems that function more bureaucratically and less effectively in meeting people's needs. "Much of what we do is already communism," Graeber surmised, "so just expand it."[93] Good advice. This additional, partial definition of capitalism as a shitty way of organizing communism that Graeber gave us also offers tinder for the applied and transformative imagination. Comprehending capital's dependence on and systematic abuse of human community and comradery could be a precondition for overcoming our own dependence on domination, exploitation, and bureaucracy.

Moreover, the contrarian historical research Graeber did with collaborator David Wengrow evinced how prehistoric and early agricultural societies both often cycled back and forth on a seasonal basis between hierarchical forms of organization and egalitarian organizational

> **When disaster strikes, mutual aid often further displaces hierarchical and authoritarian systems that function more bureaucratically and less effectively in meeting people's needs.**

forms.[94] At some point, the hierarchies solidified. We do not have to accept the assumed inevitability of the trajectory we took. Nor should we let extant bureaucracies obstructing the humanizing imagination trick us into thinking the present state of affairs immutable. Graeber and Wengrow invited us to check our preconceptions and prejudices to entertain the evidence indicating participatory democracy and egalitarian social relations have been quite commonplace in cities and even in expansive confederacies throughout history.

Currents of reactionary and proto-fascist thought operating during this period of interlocking crises believe a civil war in the US is fast approaching and, some contend, even desirable.

Less common historically, Graeber and Wengrow acknowledged, has been egalitarian family and household life. "Once the historical verdict is in," they wrote, "we will see that the most painful loss of human freedoms began at the small scale – the level of gender relations, age groups, and domestic servitude – the kind of relationships that contain at once the greatest intimacy and the deepest forms of structural violence."[95] In addition to the ongoing significance of the '68 slogans quoted above, the old feminist adage that "the personal is the political" appears equally apropos for the current conjuncture, if we engage with Graeber and Wengrow in good faith. They even predicted that it is in those smaller scale domestic and personal spaces "where the most difficult work of creating a free society will have to take place."[96] I predict that it is also in those spaces where a key component of abolitionist (and abolition feminist) strategy can find fertile ground. Such strategies likely call for a pedagogical reimagining of the values we instill in youth and efforts to teach and learn "justice" outside of the reigning punitive and retributive paradigms. Bureaucratic models of justice have hitherto justified state terror, racist policing, and the obscenity of plucking people out of communities to lock them in cages (further damaging those communities in the process).

The established structures of domination pervert our imaginative potential, insidiously promoting identification with the forces responsible for enforcing asinine behaviors and for maintaining an order predicated upon them. We can refuse to play the role of bureaucrats. We can attempt to ascertain "the real relation of those domains of life artificially separated into 'economics,' 'politics,' and 'ecology'"[97] instead of simply accepting without question the abstract notions of economic value. Examining the world anew is critical because hegemonic value elides what we know (and Graeber knew) to be of far superior value – our mutual constitution and the imagination involved in cooperatively making one another.

Graeber's ideas took concrete form in the Occupy Wall Street movement he helped get off the ground – one of the recent movements he deemed a viable experiment "in what a genuinely non-bureaucratized social order, based on the power of practical imagination, might look like."[98] Graeber also equipped us with the intellectual fuel needed to think beyond what prevails at present. He outlined frameworks for informing and catalyzing emergent exercises in opening up the horizon of possibility to actualize the collective potential of our imagination. The onus is upon us to use his gift going forward. Ⓐ

James Anderson is an adjunct professor working in Southern California. He is from Illinois but now tries each semester to cobble together classes to teach at various Southern California colleges and universities. He also taught a class at the California Rehabilitation Center as part of the Norco College prison education program. In addition, he has worked as a freelance writer for several outlets.

An earlier version of this essay appeared on the Institute for Anarchist Studies website.

Endnotes

1   David Graeber, "Dead Zones of the Imagination: An Essay on Structural Stupidity," in *The Utopia of Rules: On Technology, Stupidity, and the Secret Joys of Bureaucracy* (Brooklyn, NY: Melville House, 2015), 45-47.

2   Graeber. "Dead Zones of the Imagination," 48.

3   I gave a talk a few years back critically grappling with some of the points in that "Dead Zones" essay. I did so by considering Graeber's arguments in relation to higher education. To modify a sage aphorism slightly, critical reflection can be the highest form of flattery – and it can pave the road to greater understanding. Despite disagreeing with some of what he wrote, I nevertheless learned a lot from his work; I have learned even more upon reexamining what he wrote, and I have revised some of my previous thoughts as a result.

4   Graeber, "Dead Zones of the Imagination," 90.

5   Ibid.

6   David Graeber, "The Iron Law of Liberalism and the Era of Total Bureaucratization," *The Utopia of Rules: On Technology, Stupidity, and the Secret Joys of Bureaucracy* (Brooklyn, NY: Melville House, 2015), 18.

7   Graeber, "Dead Zones of the Imagination," 83.

8 Ibid.

9 Graeber, "The Iron Law of Liberalism and the Era of Total Bureaucratization," 9.

10 Graeber, "Dead Zones of the Imagination," 57.

11 David Graeber, "Turning Modes of Production Inside Out: Or, Why Capitalism is a Transformation of Slavery," *Critique of Anthropology* 26, no. 1 (2006): 76.

12 Graeber, "Dead Zones of the Imagination," 67.

13 Ibid., 70.

14 Graeber, "Turning Modes of Production Inside Out," 76.

15 Ibid.

16 David Graeber, *Debt: The First 5,000 Years* (Brooklyn, NY: Melville House, 2011), 29.

17 Graeber, "Turning Modes of Production Inside Out," 76.

18 David Graeber, "Revolution in Reverse," in *Revolutions in Reverse: Essays on Politics, Violence, Art, and Imagination* (Brooklyn, NY: Autonomedia, 2011), 48.

19 Graeber, "Revolution in Reverse," 48.

20 Michael Albert, "An Introduction to Participatory Economics," *ZNet* (November 5, 2016).

21 David Graeber, *The Democracy Project: A History, a Crisis, a Movement* (Spiegel & Grau: New York, 2013) 283-284.

22 These criticisms of markets are drawn largely from Michael Albert, *Parecon: Life After Capitalism* (Verso: New York, 2003).

23 Graeber, "Turning Modes of Production Inside Out," 77.

24 Ibid.

25 Ibid., 77-78.

26 Graeber, "The Iron Law of Liberalism and the Era of Total Bureaucratization," 31-32.

27 Ibid., 32.

28 Ibid.

29 David Graeber, "Revolution in Reverse," 52.

30 Graeber, "Dead Zones of the Imagination," 73.

31 Ibid.

32 Ibid., 74.

33 Ibid., 80.

34 Ibid.

35 Ibid.

36 Ibid.

37 Ibid., 70. Elsewhere, Graeber explicitly credited Patricia Hill Collins, Donna Haraway, Sandra Harding, Nancy Hartsock and bell hooks with having already raised many of the same issues and with having already laid the theoretical groundwork for much of what he contributed. See: Graeber, "Revolution in Reverse," 51. In addition, I think many of Graeber's ideas discussed in this essay also reflect what a lot of abolition feminist thinkers – like Angela Davis, Ruth Wilson Gilmore and Mariame Kaba – have argued.

38 Ibid, 69.

39 Ibid.

40 Albert, Parecon, 182.

41 Alex Press, "On the Origins of the Professional-Managerial Class: An Interview with Barbara Ehrenreich," *Dissent* (October 22, 2019).

42 Graeber, "Revolution in Reverse," 54.

43 Ibid., 55.

44 Some of the examples of alienation provided in this paragraph come from the following: Arthur Asa Berger, "Marxist Analysis," in *Media Analysis Techniques*, 3rd ed. (Thousand Oaks, CA: Sage Publications, 2005), 43-72.

45 Richard Wolff, the Marxian economist who helped start the Democracy at Work social movement organization for economic democracy, is fond of saying this.

46 Graeber, "Dead Zones of the Imagination," 71.

47 Ibid., 71-72.

48 Graeber, "Turning Modes of Production Inside Out," 74.

49 Ibid., 75.

50 Ibid., 74.

51 Ibid.

52 Ibid., 70.

53 Ibid., 75.

54 Ibid.

55 Ibid.

56 Ibid., 81.

57 Ibid.

58 Ibid.

59 Noam Chomsky, *Hegemony or Survival: America's Quest for Global Dominance* (Henry Holt and Company, LLC: New York, 2003), 6.

60 Graeber, "Dead Zones of the Imagination," 83.

61 Graeber, "Revolution in Reverse," 45.

62 Graeber, "Dead Zones of the Imagination," 48.

63 Ibid., 48-49.

64 Graeber, "The Iron Law of Liberalism and the Era of Total Bureaucratization," 26.

65 Ibid.

66 Graeber, "Dead Zones of the Imagination," 88.

67 Ibid., 99.

68 Graeber, "Revolution in Reverse," 51.

69 Ibid.

70 See the following for this point about advertising: Berger, "Marxist Analysis," 59; Hans Magnus Enzensberger, *The Consciousness Industry: On Literature, Politics and the Media* (New York: Seabury, 1974), 10.

71 The brief critique in this paragraph is drawn from Berger, "Marxist Analysis".

72 Christian Fuchs, "The Political Economy of Privacy on Facebook," Television & New Media 13, no. 2 (2012): 139-159.

73 Fuchs, "The Political Economy of Privacy on Facebook," 143.

74 Graeber, "Dead Zones of the Imagination," 99.

75 Graeber, "Revolution in Reverse," 61.

76 Graeber, "Dead Zones of the Imagination," 95-96.

77 Ibid., 92.

78 Ibid.

79 Ibid., 92-93.

80 Ibid., 97.

81 Ibid., 96.

82 Ibid., 97.

83 David Graeber, *Direct Action: An Ethnography* (Oakland, CA: AK Press, 2009), 210.

84 Graeber, Direct Action, 211.

85 Ibid., 210-211.

86 David Graeber, "The Shock of Victory," *Rolling Thunder*, no. 5 (2008): 20.

87 Graeber, "The Shock of Victory," 14.

88 Cited in Rebecca Solnit, "David Graeber: Beholden," *Guernica* (May 1, 2012), para. 30.

89 The last essay Graeber co-authored was likely a foreword intended for a new release of Kropotkin's famous text; see: Andrej Grubačić, "In loving memory of our friend, comrade, and mentor… David Graeber," PM Press Blog (September 3, 2020); Peter Kropotkin, *Mutual Aid: An Illuminated Factor of Evolution* (PM Press, forthcoming).

90 David Graeber, "The Sadness of Post-Workerism," in *Revolutions in Reverse: Essays on Politics, Violence, Art, and Imagination* (Brooklyn, NY: Autonomedia, 2011), 104.

91 Cited in Solnit, "David Graeber," para. 30.

92 Ibid.

93 Ibid.

94 David Graeber and David Wengrow, "How to change the course of human history (at least, the part that's already happened," *Eurozine* (March 2, 2018).

95 Graeber and Wengrow, "How to change the course of human history," section 5, para. 8.

96 Ibid.

97 David Graeber, "Against Kamikaze Capitalism," in *Revolutions in Reverse: Essays on Politics, Violence, Art, and Imagination* (Brooklyn, NY: Autonomedia, 2011), 114.

98 Graeber, "Dead Zones of the Imagination," 100.

POPULAR POWER IN AN AGE OF PROTEST AND PANDEMIC

ENRIQUE GUERRERO-LÓPEZ & CAMERON HUGHES

AS THE DEATH TOLL FROM COVID-19 SURPASSED 100,000 IN THE United States, capturing headlines across the country, streets that had recently been quieted by a patchwork quarantine quickly filled with the sights and sounds of mass rebellion. Beginning in Minneapolis, Minnesota in response to the brutal police murder of George Floyd, protests rapidly spread to every state in the US and beyond, raising the banner of Black Lives Matter (BLM) around the world. The scale, scope, and militancy of the uprising forced a collective reckoning with some of the most profound fault lines of US society – anti-Black racism, the role of police and prisons, the limits of reform and representation, poverty and inequality, public health and safety, militarization, and more – demonstrating the power of disruptive forms of mass direct action. On the heels of what is likely the largest protest mobilization in US history[1] and in the midst of a still raging pandemic that has spurred on organizing in several key sectors, the question of *power* is now more crucial than ever. Groupings on the broader Left have deployed a range of slogans to describe their conceptions of power and how to relate to it. From "dual power," a confounding phrase that has been recently divorced from its original Leninist definition, to the "political power" often sought by electoral socialists, there are as many understandings of power as there are micro-ideological differences on the Left. Although many anarchists see power as synonymous with exploitation and domination, our view is that power is a relationship forged by the struggle between competing social forces, particularly that of the *dominant* and *dominated* classes. Despite the promise of the recent rebellion, the current balance of forces in the US remains tilted disproportionately on the side of the dominant classes. To pose a more credible threat to existing power relations, we need to build our own power in strategic sites of struggle, forming a broad-based movement capable of extracting concessions from the state and capital in the short-term, linking struggles across sectors over time, and ultimately, carrying out a social revolution toward a libertarian socialist society. For any of this to be possible however, we must first develop a solid conceptual grasp of what we, as anarchists, mean when we say the word *power*.

What Is Power?

Anarchism is often understood to be in opposition to power. As the late Murray Bookchin once wrote, "anarchists have traditionally conceived of power as a malignant evil that must be destroyed."[2] This is consistent with many of the so-called classical anarchists of the 19th century, who often associated power with the state, but anarchism neither is nor should be limited to a purely negative conception of power.

Drawing on the work of Spanish theorist Tomás Ibáñez, Brazilian anarchist Felipe Corrêa highlights three forms of power:

> **Power as capacity:** this refers to the ability or potential of a group or individual to act as a social force in a given social relationship. For example, an individual tenant has limited capacity to get their landlord to fix broken appliances. But if the same tenant gets together with their neighbors, who face the same issue and share the same landlord, to form a tenants' union, they now have a greater potential to act as a social force to address their shared problems.

> **Power as asymmetry in social relations:** this type of power has to do with the relatively unequal capacities of the different social forces in a given social relationship. For example, a small feminist group stages a sit-in at the state capital in response to recently passed legislation restricting access to abortion. Within an hour, state police arrest all members of the group and access to abortion remains restricted.

> **Power as structures and mechanisms of regulation and control:** this refers to the various structures/institutions

(capitalism, the state, schools, family, etc.) that shape existing social relations and the range of instruments (laws, police, prisons, mass media, religion, etc.) used to maintain social control within society.[3]

In this sense, power is not necessarily good or bad, but it is contingent on who is wielding it, how they're wielding it, and toward what end. According to Ibáñez, anarchists are not against power *per se*, but a particular type of power – domination.[4] At the heart of anarchist critiques of the current social order lies the rejection of domination in all its forms. Relationships of domination can be found between social classes, racialized groups, genders, and nation states, to name a few examples. These relationships are rooted in social, political, and economic institutions where the dominant classes are structurally positioned to wield power at the expense of the dominated. Capitalism, for example, creates a social relationship between capitalists, who own the means of production, and workers, who are forced to sell their labor to capitalists in order to survive. This places capitalists in a structural position of power that enables them to exploit workers, hire and fire, speed up production at the expense of the workforce, and so on. Structures and relationships of domination are fostered through a complex mix of coercion and consent, from the police baton to the ideology of "American exceptionalism."[5]

These hierarchical structures and relationships – namely capitalism, the state, heteropatriarchy, white supremacy, imperialism, and settler-colonialism – are constitutive of a mutually reinforcing system of domination.

This system of domination is deeply entrenched, but its relative power is shaped by the intensity of the ongoing conflict between the dominant classes and the dominated classes. This is why anarchists have historically favored strategies that build power from the bottom up, developing the capacity of social forces "from below" to not only challenge but ultimately uproot systems of domination. To this end, anarchist political organizations around the world have taken up the banner of building *popular power*.

What Is Popular Power?

Emerging from struggles in Latin America in the 1970s, the theory and practice of popular power has evolved with competing interpretations on the Left throughout the region. Marxist conceptions of popular power cut across the range of tendencies in Latin America, from libertarian to authoritarian currents, sometimes leaving the door open to the state. In Cuba and Venezuela, for example, popular power has become institutionalized through the national government and brought under its direct control. Among anarchists, however, popular power has become a mode of struggle and a political horizon with an orientation outside, against, and beyond the state. The *Federación Anarquista Uruguaya* (FAU) became the first political organization to articulate the anarchist strategy of building popular power,[6] which has been adopted by similar groups throughout South America and beyond.

The project of building popular power is rooted in the transformative potential of mass social movements. Throughout US history, periods of popular unrest, in which social movements have reached a critical mass, have produced the most significant social, political, and economic gains – including the weekend, dismantling Jim Crow, abortion rights, and so on – despite intense opposition from the forces of domination. Mass movements have the power to wrest reforms from the dominant classes, disrupt existing power relations, and lay the basis for a libertarian socialist society. For this reason, the project of building popular power is about developing the capacity, consciousness, and combativeness of social movements. But not all movements are created equal.

Guided by a libertarian socialist horizon, building popular power calls for social movements with a certain set of characteristics. First, this implies movements that respond to our shared material needs and interests as exploited and oppressed people (better working conditions, dignified housing, safety from state violence, etc.). To avoid the pitfalls of collaboration with the forces of domination, this approach is oriented toward autonomous social movements to maintain independence from the state, political parties, nonprofits, and other intermediary impediments to class struggle.

Beyond class independence, movements that advance popular power are democratically controlled by their members, use direct action as their primary mode of struggle, and practice popular education – building confidence, skills, and capacity for self-management. Because movements are embedded within systems of domination that divide us along lines of race, gender, nationality, and so on, struggles for popular power must be imbued with an intersectional, internationalist perspective to foster a culture of solidarity and accountability. Lastly, the strength of mass movements, in part, rests on their ability to disrupt business as usual, a notion that the recent rebellion against anti-Black state violence stands as a clear testament to. This is why we need militant mass movements willing to break with the restraining rules (whether ideological or legal) of the system of domination, in order to advance on our own terms.

For anarchists, building popular power is both a means and an end. As libertarian socialists, we envision a classless, stateless society free from domination, where people collectively control their workplaces and communities, where production and distribution are based on the principle "from each according to ability, to each according to need,"[7] and where we live sustainably with the planet in a federated system organized from the bottom up. In this vision, popular power is a lived reality throughout society. But this future society can only be brought about through a revolutionary rupture with the status quo. This is why we are committed to building independent, self-managed, and militant mass movements as organs of popular power that both reflect a new society and act as a vehicle for its realization.

How Do We Build Popular Power In The Current Moment?

The project of building popular power faces a mix of obstacles and opportunities in the current conjuncture. Circumstances imposed by the ongoing global pandemic have put many workers, particularly workers of color, in a desperate situation. Unemployment is the highest it's been since the Great Depression,[8] leaving many unable to pay rent or cover monthly bills. Those who have been able to keep their jobs as "essential workers" continue to face unsafe working conditions, with thousands contracting the virus at work. Due to the particularities of racial capitalism, the pandemic has disproportionately affected Black, non-Black Latinx, and Indigenous populations, leading to higher death rates and deepening social and economic inequality.[9] These conditions have been disorienting, at times paralyzing, but they have also lifted the veil on entrenched inequalities and the failure of capital and the state to meet our needs, inspiring a wave of radicalization and revolt around the country, both fueling and fueled by the BLM rebellion.

The militancy of the uprising against white supremacy and police brutality, expressed in burning police cars and precincts, toppled statues, broken curfews, and clashes with police, dramatically reshaped the terrain of class struggle in the US. But the forces of counterinsurgency, from the Democratic Party to the nonprofit industrial complex, moved with a quickness to pacify the movement, achieving mixed results in the process.

Now that the movement has withdrawn from the streets, we must, as revolutionary anarchists, provide a compelling answer to the perennial question, "Where do we go from here?"

To address this question, we need to look closely at what sectors of society offer the most potential for developing popular power.

Actors Of Struggle, Sites Of Struggle

The shifting balance of forces that marks the current moment calls for a clear strategy which both consolidates and builds off of existing struggles. This will require building popular power across multiple sites of struggle that are anchored by concrete *actors of struggle*. According to Chilean anarchist José Antonio Gutiérrez D., actors of struggle are defined by:

1. Problems that affect them immediately and their immediate interests,

2. Traditions of struggle and organization that emerge from these problems and interests,

3. A common place or activity in society. [10]

In Latin America, traditional actors of struggle have been workers, students, neighbors, and peasants, each associated with a specific *sector* or *site of struggle* where class conflict takes concrete form: workplaces, schools, neighborhoods and territories, etc. The US has a rich history of social movement activity associated with all these actors of struggle, except for peasants. Given the defining role of prisons in the US, coupled with the long tradition of struggle and organization in this sector, we believe prisoners, rather than peasants, represent a critical actor of struggle. Therefore prisons, alongside workplaces, schools, and neighborhoods/territories, constitute strategic sites of struggle for building popular power in the US.

Each of these sectors are intimately interlinked. A wage cut affects our ability to pay our rent or mortgage. If housing and income become an ongoing issue, this may affect whether or not we will be able to pursue an education. This, in turn, could prevent us from meeting the terms of our parole. In other words, isolating specific sites of struggle does not entail viewing them in isolation, but instead allows us to focus our efforts on where and how class conflict is taking shape, while also clarifying how each sector is marked by structures, relations, and instruments of domination.

We have seen the potential of all these sites of struggle in the current moment. In the midst of the pandemic, nurses, Amazon workers, and others have organized hundreds of work stoppages and other actions to protect their health and safety, building off of two years of increased strike activity, the most we have seen since the 1980s.[11] High school students have become increasingly militant, mobilizing to kick cops out of their schools as part of the broader BLM movement. Neighborhood-based or territorial struggles have taken on a variety of forms, from popular assemblies and mutual aid networks, to tenant unions organizing rent strikes. In spite of deeply repressive and dangerous conditions, people in jails, prisons, and detention centers have risen up in response to the coronavirus and under the banner of BLM, staging hunger strikes, escaping from facilities, and refusing orders from armed guards.

The fight against police brutality and white supremacy has demonstrated the potency of weaving together these sites of struggle into a broader multi-sectoral movement with solidarity as the glue. In Minneapolis and New York City, unionized bus drivers refused to transport arrested protesters to jail.[12] On Juneteenth, the International Longshore and Warehouse Union shut down West Coast ports in solidarity with the George Floyd uprising.[13] The Los Angeles Tenants Union has tied the call to "defund the police" to the need for social housing.[14] Educators and parents have joined students in the demand to get cops off campus.[15] Immigrant detainees in an ICE detention facility in California staged a hunger strike in solidarity with George Floyd.[16]

There Are Levels To It (Political, Social, And Intermediate)

Developing a multi-sectoral strategy for building popular power entails different forms of organization, a clear understanding of the unique role of each of these forms, and an analysis of the relationship between them in the course of struggle. Since the late 19th century, social anarchists have developed a theory and practice of "dual organization"[17] that emphasizes the need for both a *political level* and a *social level* of distinct but complementary types of organization.

The political level of organization brings together anarchist militants who share a common ideological perspective and political program. This level requires a high degree of political and tactical unity and is aimed at cultivating a "militant minority"[18] of revolutionaries to engage in collective analysis and strategy, active involvement in movements, and political education in and outside of the organization. Anarchist political organizations are composed of various actors of struggle (workers, students, neighbors, etc.), and their members participate in social movements as rank-and-file militants dedicated to defending and expanding the revolutionary potential of the working class, not as a parasitic force seeking to co-opt struggles for its own benefit. As Black Rose/Rosa Negra points out in our "Role of the Revolutionary Organization":

> The revolutionary organization should be a tool for the active and militant members within the class. It never seeks to dominate, impose upon, manipulate, command or control mass movements in recognition of the need for revolutionary pluralism, and that those movements, not the revolutionary organization itself, are the revolutionary agent of social transformation.[19]

Social level organizations, on the other hand, bring together actors of struggle (workers, tenants, students, etc.), who are situated in a particular sector or site of struggle (the workplace, the neighborhood/territory, schools and universities), in order to address their concrete needs through collective action. Examples of social level organizations include labor unions, tenant unions, militant student organizations, and so on.

It's important to note that social level organizations, unlike those of the political level, gather actors of struggle with a variety of different ideological perspectives. This level of organization aims to unify as many actors of struggle as possible and build our capacity to impose our demands and gain increasing amounts of ground from the dominant classes.

As anarchists organized at the political level, one of our main priorities is to create and/or expand social level organizations. As rank-and-file participants, we promote our values, principles, and practices from within mass movements, combat reformist and vanguardist currents, and expose the contradictions of capital, the state, and social domination.

But it is not a one-way street. As anarchists, we don't organize ourselves to impose our politics as some kind of removed alien force within social level organizations. We, too, are members of the dominated classes, and as such, we are directly invested in building the capacity of popular organizations to address our material needs. Our experience in mass struggles informs our theoretical and political development, which we are then able to take back into social movements in a mutually reinforcing and complementary relationship.

Despite recent movement activity, social level organizations remain underdeveloped in the US. For example, roughly ten percent of workers belong to unions,[20] primarily in the public sector, meaning the vast majority of workers are unorganized. Because of this, we need the political level to develop militants committed to building social level formations within the sites of struggle identified above. This task often requires starting at a third *intermediate level*, found between the political and social levels, to lay the foundation for mass movement.

Like those found on the social level, intermediate level organizations also bring together actors situated in a common site of struggle but are typically smaller in size and driven by a shared political orientation. An example we might look to is the mutual aid networks that emerged in the wake of the pandemic, which have brought together neighbors from various backgrounds to meet each other's needs in a way that promotes autonomy, solidarity, and direct democracy.[21] The intermediate level can also be found within long standing movements, often promoting a distinct set of politics and course of action within a broader formation. We can see this in the Caucus of Rank-and-file Educators (CORE)[22] in the Chicago Teachers Union, which played a key role in organizing Chicago's last two public education strikes and has been a force for severing ties between Chicago Public Schools and the local police department.[23]

During periods of widespread radicalization, such as the one we've recently lived through, the potential for intermediate level organizations

KARA LYNCH AKA LOVEYBOI AS STAR, *NO TITLE*

to transition into mass social movements can be accelerated. Ultimately, though, all three levels – political, intermediate, and social – will play a critical role in building power from below.

Conclusion

The anarchist movement in North America (and elsewhere), while experiencing a surprising resurgence in the last 30 years, has suffered from an underdeveloped repertoire of analytic and strategic tools. Facing a highly complex world marred by compounding and accelerating crises, it's incumbent on anarchists to develop our ability to critically and systematically analyze the balance of forces in a given moment, so that we can determine where and how to most effectively intervene. The concepts elucidated in this writing – of power, actors and sites of struggle, and levels of organization – are informed by decades of practical experience accrued by anarchist militants around the world and provide a working model for analysis that is already being put into use.

Recent rebellions against unabated racist state violence and an economic logic that demands the continued circulation of capital in the midst of a deadly pandemic have demonstrated that, while raw force can tip the scales briefly, a permanent re-ordering of social relations requires long-term revolutionary strategy and organization. Ⓐ

Notes

1   Between 15,000,000 and 26,000,000 US adults took part in protests related to the murder of George Floyd. "Civis Analytics," *Coronavirus Pulse Survey Research*, (Chicago: Civisanalytics.com, 2020).

2   Murray Bookchin. "Anarchism, Power, and Government," *New Compass*, (January 2014).

3   Felipe Corrêa, "Anarchism, Power, Class, and Social Change," *Em Debate* no. 8 (2012), doi:10.5007/1980-3532.2012n8p69.

4   Tomás Ibáñez, *Poder y Libertad* (Barcelona: Hora, 1982).

5   *American exceptionalism* is the notion that the United States of America is somehow qualitatively different from, and therefore superior to, all other nations.

6   Federación Anarquista Uruguaya, "Poder Popular desde lo Libertario," May 15, 2020.

7   Karl Marx, *Critique of the Gotha Programme*, Stuttgart, *Die Neue Zeit*, 1875.

8   US Bureau of Labor Statistics, *May 2020 Employment Situation News Release*, USDL-20-0815, (Washington, D.C.: BLS, 2020).

9   American Public Media Research Lab, *The Color of Coronavirus: COVID-19 Deaths by Race and Ethnicity in the US*, (St. Paul, Minnesota: American Public Media, 2020).

10 José Antonio Gutiérrez D., "The Problems Posed by the Concrete Class Struggle and Popular Organization," *Black Rose/Rosa Negra Anarchist Federation Blog*, September 19, 2017.

11 Andrew Keshner, "Strikes are 257% Up in 2 Years, Even Though Labor Union Membership is Down – Why More Workers are Taking a Stand," *Marketwatch*, February 13, 2020.

12 Madeleine Carlisle, "Bus Drivers in Minneapolis and New York City Have Refused to Help With Police Transportation," *Time Magazine*, May 30, 2020.

13 International Longshore & Warehouse Union, "ILWU Stands Down at West Coast Ports for Historic Juneteenth Action to Honor Black lives," *ILWU Website*, July 13, 2020.

14 Tyler Kingkade, "Los Angeles Activists Were Already Pushing to Defund the Police. Then George Floyd Died," *NBC News*, June 15, 2020.

15 Mark Keierleber, "Teachers Unions Historically Supported Campus Cops. George Floyd's Death – and a Wave of 'Militant' Educator Activists – Forced Them to Reconsider," *The 74 Million*, July 27, 2020.

16 Fernie Ortiz, "ICE Now Says Detainees Held Hunger Strike in Honor of George Floyd," *Border Report,* June 10, 2020.

17 Davide Turcato, "Italian Anarchism as a Transnational Movement, 1885–1915," *International Review of Social History* 52, no. 3 (2007): 407–44. doi:10.1017/S0020859007003057.

18 Micah Uetricht and Barry Eidlin, "U.S. Union Revitalization and the Missing 'Militant Minority,'" *Labor Studies Journal* 44, no. 1 (March 2019): 36–59, doi:10.1177/0160449X19828470.

19 Black Rose/Rosa Negra Anarchist Federation, "Role of the Revolutionary Organization," 2014.

20 US Bureau of Labor Statistics, *January 2020 Union Members Summary,* USDL-20-0108 (Washington, D.C.: BLS, 2020).

21 Jia Tolentino, "What Mutual Aid Can Do During a Pandemic," *New Yorker,* May 11, 2020.

22 Peter Brogan, "Getting to the CORE of the Chicago Teachers' Union Transformation," *Studies in Social Justice* 8, no. 2 (2014): 145-164, doi:10.26522/ssj.v8i2.1031.

23 Indigo Olivier, "Chicago Teachers Join the Nationwide Movement to Kick Cops Out of Schools," *In These Times,* June 17, 2020.

***Enrique Guerrero-López** is a member of the Black Rose/Rosa Negra Anarchist Federation, a public high school teacher, and rank-and-file union militant in North Carolina. eguerrerolopez109@gmail.com*

***Cameron Hughes** is a member of the Black Rose/Rosa Negra Anarchist Federation in the California Bay Area, a teaching assistant, and a rank-and-file union militant in UAW 2865. camhughes@ucsc.edu*

Chemical weapons contaminate skin, hair, clothing, and anything you are carrying.

ASPER

SO YOU GOT TEARGASSED?
HERBAL SELF-CARE AFTER EXPOSURE TO CHEMICAL WEAPONS

MISSY ROHS

IF 2020 BROUGHT ANYTHING TO MY HOMETOWN OF PORTLAND, OREGON, it was the opportunity to be exposed to chemical weapons. Protesters, residents both housed and unhoused, bystanders, and workers throughout the city have been caught off guard by law enforcement's prolific deployment of tear gas, pepper spray, and the like. Sometimes, the surprise has been in the timing or quantity – but other times, the chemical weapons (CW) used have changed from night to night, with differing colors or distinct effects. These tactics serve to spread fear and alarm, dissuading people from participating in the resistance.

For those of us on the ground, the treatment and decontamination procedures for these CW remain more or less the same, regardless of the specific substance used. And when it comes to aftercare, symptoms dictate the course of action far more than the chemical composition of the toxins does. This piece is about aftercare: what to do in the hours, days, and weeks following your CW exposure once you've decontaminated and completed any necessary first aid interventions. Let's sort it out by symptom, then, shall we?

MEDICINAL PLANTS
FOR CHEMICAL WEAPONS EXPOSURE

Marsh-mallow

Dandelion

Mullein

Comfrey

Skullcap

Chamomile

Yarrow

Lavender

[Before we get any further: Consider seeing a licensed health care practitioner as soon as possible if you are injured or exposed to CW as a result of police action. If you have lingering effects of CW or end up in a legal battle with the state, this kind of documentation can be very useful in the long run. In addition, licensed nurse practitioners, doctors, and other primary care practitioners can use their diagnostic tools to rule out serious zmedical issues stemming from your CW exposure or protest injuries. Call on mutual aid networks if things like money, transportation, or childcare are the only issues keeping you from needed health care. Your wellbeing is worth it!]

Dry, irritated respiratory tract
Sore throat, dry cough, lung soreness, painful sinuses, dry eyes

Dry conditions call for lubricating the mucosa. My favorite suggestion for this is to find a couple boxes of a tea blend with a name like "throat soother" or "throat coat" at the local natural foods store – they're sure to contain moistening herbs like marshmallow (*Althaea officinalis*), violet (*Viola* spp.), and licorice (*Glycyrrhiza* spp.). You can also make your own tea blend of these herbs! I like to double up on tea bags, letting the infusion steep for a couple of hours when possible. Eating slimy foods like okra, chia seeds, or nopales is also a great (and delicious!) way to moisten respiratory tissue.

Inflamed or congested respiratory tract
Lung soreness, snotty sinuses, any cough, sore throat

Pretty much anyone who is exposed to CW will have some respiratory tract inflammation. For this, my go-to tonic is mullein leaf (*Verbascum thapsus*). This common plant is difficult for novices to identify, with some toxic look-alikes, but is easy and sustainable to grow and harvest – a worthwhile herbal remedy to get to know. It can be used as a tincture (plant material extracted into an alcohol base) or a tea. To make your own tea, grab a large handful of chopped dried or fresh mullein leaves, pour a quart of near-boiling water over it, cover, and let steep for a minimum of twenty minutes. When you're ready to drink your mullein infusion, pour through a fine filter – a coffee filter or old cotton tshirt work well – as mullein has very small hairs that can irritate the throat if not strained out. As the tea can taste bland, feel free to use sweetener and creamer as desired.

Another way to increase the palatability of mullein tea is to add an aromatic herb to the mix. This can be literally any plant that has a strong scent and a pleasant-to-you taste – think peppermint, lemongrass, cinnamon, or rosemary, for example. Aromatic plants not only help things taste good; they play an important role in CW recovery by acting as gentle expectorants. To that end, ingesting aromatic plants, whether in tea or in any other form, is a great idea to support the respiratory system. Eating aromatic and spicy foods like pesto, *tom kha*, or a picante salsa means ingesting volatile oils. When those volatile oils *leave* our bodies, one of the main ways they do that is through the respiratory system. On their way out, those aromatics gently irritate the mucosa that lines our airways, loosening it for excretion. Long story short, some of those CWs that you inhaled were trapped in your respiratory lining; drinking a warming chai or chowing down on some spicy greens will help you cough them back out.

All this respiratory tissue that I've been going on about? It functions best when it's humid. If it's dry out, consider running a humidifier or simmering a pot of water on the stove to moisten the air that you're breathing. Or simply take as many steamy showers as you can handle. You can combine this intervention with aromatic herbs, of course; that water bubbling away on the stove can have a scoop of thyme, fir needles, orange peels, or lavender. With this, you're humidifying the air, exposing your respiratory system to aromatics, and – wait for it – you're also calming your nervous system by inhaling volatile oils from plants. Elegant aftercare, am I right?

Eliminatory systems support
Toxin exposure

Everyone who gets a dose of CWs should be thinking about supporting their eliminatory systems: digestion, kidneys, liver, lymph, lungs, and skin. This *doesn't* look like a harsh detox

Personal Steams

1 large pot of water
1–3 handfuls of aromatic herbs
Comfy seating, bedsheet, stirring spoon, and hot pads

Bring the water to a boil. While that's happening, set up a comfortable place to sit close to the floor: a pillow or short stool works well. Lay down a protective trivet in front of the pillow to place your hot pot on. When the water boils, set the pot on the trivet, take a seat, and cover both your body and the pot with the bedsheet. Add aromatic herbs such as eucalyptus, culinary sage, lemon balm, or douglas fir to the hot water and stir. Inhale, taking care to not burn yourself with the steam. Enjoy your portable sauna for five to twenty minutes. Afterward, you may put the herbs and water back on the stove and simmer throughout the day, adding humidity and plant aromatics to your home.

diet, fasting, or anything extreme. What this *does* look like is some corny public service announcement for healthy living, or maybe an ad for a bougie spa retreat. Drink plenty of fluids – water, broth, herbal tea, coconut water, and other non-caffeinated, non-sugary, non-alcoholic drinks. Eat a rainbow of foods, with special emphasis on vegetables.

Homeland Security police used "green gas" against demonstrators in Portland – a chemical that the military stopped using in the 1990s due to its extreme toxicity.

Beans, whole grains, kale smoothies, chia seeds, and oatmeal are some of my favorite high-fiber foods to help carry toxins out of the body efficiently. Move your body: stretching, biking, yoga, silly dances, and relaxing walks in nature are all sound ideas. Sweat: saunas, cardio exercise, and hot baths can do the trick. Sleep as much as your body wants (aim for eight to ten hours if you can), at night when possible. Go easy on the sugar, alcohol, smoking, over-the-counter painkillers, and other drugs that you use, if feasible. Gentle massage and dry-brushing with motions toward the heart both give excellent support to the lymphatic system.

Liver support
Acne, hives, menstrual dysregulation, hormone imbalance, night sweats

There are a lot of one-size-fits-all recommendations floating around about herbs to support the liver and hormones after CW exposure. In my experience, there are few herbs that fit everyone across the board for these issues, and some liver- and hormone-supporting herbs can cause irritability, nausea, menstrual flooding, and other undesirable symptoms when taken by a person whose constitution doesn't match the herb. Ideally, each individual would consult an experienced herbalist about such a protocol. In the meantime, there are some practices to support all kinds of bodies.

First of all, everything listed under "eliminatory systems support": *Do that.* Focus on hydration, high-fiber foods, plenty of sleep at night, and avoiding alcohol and painkillers (like acetaminophen and

ibuprofen) to whatever extent possible. If you like beets, beet greens, and chard, they are really supportive to liver function, so load up on borscht and feta-beet salads. Eat bitter foods (radicchio, dandelion greens, artichokes), try bitter teas (roasted chicory and dandelion root are classics), and avoid greasy food like chips and fries. When it comes to liver-supporting herbs, I recommend consulting with an herbalist, but if that's inaccessible, folks with skin symptoms such as acne or hives might want to try a tincture of burdock (*Arctium lappa, A. minus*) root or seed. Those with menstrual and hormonal irregularities may find that dandelion root (*Taraxacum officinale*), yellow dock root (*Rumex crispus*), or artichoke leaf (*Cynara scolymus*) may be a key part of an herbal formula. And those who are returning to the streets, or otherwise risking further CW exposure, might decide to take milk thistle seed (*Silybum marianum*) as a tincture or in capsules to protect the liver.

Digestive issues
Sudden nausea, vomiting, cramping gut, loose stools

There have been nights in Portland when large portions of protesters who were exposed to CWs experienced extreme nausea or sudden vomiting. This symptom picture is disconcerting on its own; the fact that it was a *different* symptom picture than in days and weeks past would inspire me to seek professional medical attention if I were one of the people affected – CW use like that may be the subject of legal action, and if so, would need all the substantiating documentation it could get. Word on the street was that people were being encouraged to consume activated charcoal if they experienced vomiting. Unfortunately, this advice misses the mark: activated charcoal grabs onto toxins (and nourishing food) *in the digestive system* when it's consumed and carries them out of the body before they can be digested. However, activated charcoal does nothing for toxins that were inhaled or absorbed through the skin, which is how CWs at protests are deployed. In cases like this, taking activated charcoal can do more harm than good, since it blocks the absorption and effects of any food or vitamins or medicines in the stomach while doing nothing to mitigate the harm that the CWs are causing. The best approach for digestive upset in such cases, barring any medical professional's recommendations, is once again to support the eliminatory systems so that your body can process and clear the CWs as efficiently as possible. Vomiting or diarrhea additionally call for rehydration: plentiful water with electrolytes, whether in the form of coconut water, gatorade, or the World Health Organization's rehydration formula.

Home Rehydration Formula

1 quart (or liter) water
1/2 tsp table salt
2 Tbsp sugar

Mix ingredients together and sip. This combo can be flavored by replacing the water with herbal tea (ginger or peppermint are both anti-nausea), stock/broth (subtract the salt if the broth already has sodium), or a diluted juice (reduce or eliminate sugar as needed).

Wounds
Minor burns, bruises, scrapes

Minor burns, once cooled and cleaned, benefit greatly from aloe gel (*Aloe vera, Aloe spp.*) applied topically. Both the fresh leaves (often found at groceries catering to Central American communities) yield gel that cools the area and promotes healing. Alternately, a compress of chilled tea of rose petals (*Rosa spp.*) or lavender flowers (*Lavandula spp.*) can be applied with a clean cloth to the burn to astringe the skin and provide mild pain relief. Hold the moist cloth to the burn for ten to twenty minutes, three to four times per day.

Minor bruises and scrapes can be treated with compresses as above, tinctures applied topically, or infused oils gently rubbed into the area. Wound-healing herbs like calendula flowers (*Calendula officinalis*), plantain (*Plantago major* & *P. lanceolata*), and yarrow leaves and flowers (*Achillea millefolium*) are excellent choices for all of these applications. All three grow easily in temperate climates and are commonly found in shops that carry medicinal herbs. Avoid using comfrey (*Symphytum officinale*) unless under the care of an experienced herbalist. Monitor all wounds for signs of infection: increasing heat, tenderness, swelling; smelly pus; fever; and unexplained fatigue are some of the common symptoms to watch for.

Insomnia
Trouble falling or staying asleep

Sleep disturbances are a common reaction to ongoing stress and recent emotional trauma. It's a symptom that asks us to take care of our emotional selves (see below) as much as we take care of our physical selves. In addition to generally supporting emotional, mental, and spiritual wellbeing, there are a lot of great tools for promoting sound sleep. The most basic is a wind-down ritual before bed. That can look like turning off screens for an hour before sleep, engaging in a mindfulness practice, reading a book, snuggling with human or animal loved ones, or gentle stretches, among other things. Sleep hygiene tools can help some people, too: not eating for a few hours before bed, ensuring that the bedroom is dark and quiet, using earplugs or eye masks, or sleeping alone are all possible interventions.

There are many safe and reliable herbs for sleep support. Two of my favorites are chamomile (*Matricaria chamomila*) and lavender (*Lavandula spp.*). Chamomile takes many people by surprise – they're used to small tea bags of old, dusty herb that, when brewed, taste kinda lukewarm and bland. But recently dried chamomile flowers, sourced from a top-notch herbal company or a local farmer, can create a strong tea that is fruity, buttery, floral, and surprisingly sleep-inducing. Just like the mullein tea above, you'll want to grab a large handful of dried or fresh chamomile flowers, pour a quart of hot water over the plant material, cover, and let steep for at least twenty minutes. Sweeten as desired. You'll end up with a soporific brew that knocks most folks out. Chamomile can also be taken as a tincture, or you can even make a very strong tea and add it to a bath, soaking up the medicinal constituents through your skin.

Lavender makes a great bath as well, though a strong lavender tea is likely too bitter to drink much of. Enjoy an evening soak, or use lavender either in tincture form or as an herbal sachet. Lavender works directly on the brain when smelled, which sends signals to the entire body to chill out and relax. This sachet technique can be used in the streets, as well, to calm down after a stressful experience.

Eo's Lavender Sachets

1 pint dried lavender flowers
1 pair of cheap pantyhose

This extremely economical lavender pillow was originally created for use at protests. Take about 1/4 cup of lavender flowers, tuck it into the end of the pantyhose, and tie a knot to secure the pouch. Cut the pantyhose, make a new knot, and repeat the process. To use the sachet, simply rub it and inhale the aroma. Lavender's volatile oils encourage relaxation, whether before bedtime or during a hectic demonstration.

ASPER

A sample of debris from "less-lethal" weapons used by Portland police against demonstrators during the 2020 uprising.

Nervous system support
Anxiety, post-traumatic stress, depression, circular thoughts

It is absolutely normal to have symptoms of this nature after experiencing CWs. In fact, people can experience trauma reactions even if they weren't attacked directly. Trauma reactions can happen to witnesses, friends and family of survivors, those who had close calls, and even folks who were exposed to the trauma through media or social media. It's also totally okay *not* to have a trauma reaction after CW exposure. Every person is unique. If you experience symptoms of depression, post-traumatic stress syndrome, anxiety, or any emotional or mental symptom that interferes with your day-to-day life, it's important to get professional support in addition to taking care of yourself. Talk therapy, EMDR therapy, mindfulness practices, and pastoral/spiritual guidance are just some of the options.

There are also some fantastic herbs that support the nervous system, providing both physical and emotional support through stressful times. Milky oats (*Avena sativa*) are one of my very favorites. When taken fresh in tincture form, milky oats nourish the nerves, providing a grounded, centered feeling and spreading a sense of calm. A safe and reliable tonic, milky oats are my top choice for folks who are prone to panic attacks or who feel frazzled or disembodied. Skullcap (*Scutellaria lateriflora*) is another great nerve tonic – again, best taken as a fresh-plant tincture – that helps to chill out and relax. Skullcap is a great pick for folks with tight shoulders and an inability to rest. Both of these plant allies are wonderful to take for weeks or months as part of a nervous system rejuvenation protocol, but they also work in the moment when a deep breath is needed.

In the streets and beyond:

Fight the power and do no harm!

When we take care of ourselves and take care of each other, we nourish a stronger base for creating change. Don't overlook the benefits of aftercare – both our bodies and our spirits need tending when we come up against state violence. It may be tempting to operate continuously at 110 percent during times of civil uprising, but any successful push for change is long and, at times, grueling; prepare to be in it for the long haul, and please don't burn out.

The street medic collective I was in, the Black Cross Health Collective, had as our motto, "Fight the power and do no harm!" In that spirit, only implement the ideas in this article if they feel good for your body, and if they aren't contraindicated for you. Consult your health care provider or a knowledgeable herbalist if you have a health condition or if you have any questions about your aftercare. And then, once you're recharged and well, step back in and cause some good trouble! Ⓐ

TEAR GAS IN YOUR NEIGHBORHOOD

You are currently residing within one mile of a Portland Police Bureau building. This means that you will most likely be subjected to tear gas, flash bangs, and LRAD devices.

The PPB will give you no warning and will not protect you.

We must take care of one another.

COMMON SIDE EFFECTS

Tear gas can cause coughing, shortness of breath, heightened lung problems, delayed menstruation, miscarriages, stillbirths, damages to the heart and liver, and death (in cases of extreme exposure or those with pre-existing respiratory conditions).

WHAT TO DO (AT HOME)

Turn off external AC units.
Close your windows and doors.
Remove any outside furniture (including toys & pet related objects).
Tear gas can contaminate food, clothing, and furniture for up to 72 hours.

FOR MORE INFORMATION:	We implore you to join this fight against the PPB who have been inflicting violence and trauma against the Black community with impunity and have now taken to brutalizing the people of this city. Stand up for what is right.
local medical info: @pdxactionmedics	
health and at-home care: @frontlinemedics	
community & legal resources: @dontshootpdx	
independent/local media: @defendpdx	

WE, THE PEOPLE OF PORTLAND, DEMAND THE COMPLETE AND ABSOLUTE ABOLISHMENT OF THE PPB.

BLACK LIVES MATTER

Flyer distributed by activists to warn people when the air in their neighborhoods was inundated with police chemical weapons.

Missy Rohs is a community herbalist in Portland, Oregon. These days, she channels her lifelong passion for education and rabblerousing into the Arctos School of Herbal & Botanical Studies (https://arctosschool.org/). Missy believes in the power of weeds and the importance of community.

POWER WITHIN

CINDY CRABB

"We are in such an unprecedented moment of global uprisings that fall against the backdrop of a global pandemic which is against the backdrop of institutionalized and historical racism and racialized oppression in this country and across the world. In the midst of that, we are trying to figure out how do we transform ourselves and our communities to make more room for justice in the world.... We can ground in the present moment but that doesn't mean that we don't act, that doesn't mean we don't move. We are not looking for a practice that is going to take us out of engagement with the world and engagement with our offering [but rather] a practice that is going to allow us to be with what is, to settle into this moment so we can perceive more choices; we can have a more embodied, a more daring vision for the world we can build."

Prentis Hemphill, *Somatic Centering* (IGTV)

Power Within

LIKE ALL ANIMALS, OUR BODIES ARE BIOLOGICALLY DESIGNED to respond to threat, and once the threat is over, return to homeostasis. Each organ and neural circuit, each molecule and cell, are part of an involuntary self-regulating process by which the body attempts to maintain stability while adjusting to conditions in the outside world – moment by moment for optimal survival. The stability it desires is not one of stagnation, but of dynamic equilibrium, continuous change, and maximization of the power within.

We are also designed for mobilization. When we sense a threat, our bodies move into action. The cue for mobilization often begins with a startle response – the body goes slightly stiff and still, while the eyes and pupils widen to expand our peripheral vision. Blood flow moves away from the limbs into the core, heart rate elevates, and breathing shallows in preparation for fight or flight. Next, we orient. In the wild, mammals begin the orienting process by scanning the distance. If there is no identifiable threat, they then turn their attention closer. If a threat is identified, the body goes into action. The blood moves quickly into the limbs, giving a sudden burst of energy for running, fighting or defending. This all happens involuntarily. If fight or flight is not possible, we freeze. When a body is frozen, a predator may lose interest or we may be overlooked. The next line of self-preservation is a type of stillness called dorsal vagal – the body slows way down and blood flow decreases to minimize potential blood loss. Pain receptors also deaden. And there is a detachment from the self.

In the wild, when mammals are once free of the threat, they rejoin their group, shake it off, pronk – jump up and down – to disperse the excess adrenaline, and, eventually, reorient and then return to alert, but relaxed, state of aliveness and a sense of relative safety.

Humans are driven by the same innate survival mechanisms. The mobilization or conservation of power within our bodies and the structure of each interlocking biological system strive to return to optimal stability. For the most part though, we have lost connection with the signals our bodies are giving us. The threats we face are often more complex than the body can readily comprehend. We go into overdrive or shut down and our systems are unable to process the horrors we experience, so we store the memories, feelings, and sensations as trauma. Trauma is distinct physiologically as it is stored in our short-term rather than long-term memory. This thwarts the body in its attempt to return to equilibrium.

The threats we face are often more complex than the body can readily comprehend.

Because of this, trauma often keeps our bodies and brains from being able to most effectively mobilize, even when we are dedicated to political mobilization.

I was politicized as a feminist, anarchist, and social ecologist in the late 1980s, and have been involved in organizational and street activism. For the past five years I have worked as a somatic-based therapist, supporting individuals and movement groups in understanding and processing trauma. As an activist, I have seen the effects of unprocessed trauma in our movement work. The threats we face are pervasive – white supremacy, police violence, and global capitalism, to name a few. The part of our brain that mobilizes against threat wants a specific target – something it can focus its eyes on – and when the threat is pervasive it can become overwhelmed. This is compounded by the close-up threat-inundation created by the hyper-focus our eyes go into when scanning on digital media. In fact, the body actually reads this as a threat that has crossed our innermost boundary, just inches away.

When the threat signal is immediate, relentless, and close (or perceived to be), and people don't have a solid understanding of how to work with and coax the nervous system back into regulation, people tend to see the enemy in the people who are closest. Our relationships, groups and movements devolve into fighting, blaming. Or people turn the threat inward, becoming immobilized by depression and shame. I have seen this happen in almost every organizing project I have been part of, or heard of, and I see it happening now on the streets. In the healing professions, the effects of trauma are mostly described as the following:

- **Re-experiencing** (reliving what happened, feeling like it's happening again, getting upset at reminders)
- **Avoidance** (trying to block it out and not think about it, feeling numb or no emotions)
- **Increased arousal** (always feeling afraid something bad will happen, being easily startled/jumpy, having trouble with sleep or concentration, going into fight-or-flight mode)
- **Dissociation** (feeling like everything is unreal or like a dream, having trZouble remembering parts of what happened)
- **Other** (e.g., sleep issues, appetite issues, sense of hopelessness, isolation, withdrawal from others, excessive alcohol or drug use to cope, heightened irritability with others, headaches, muscle fatigue)

In order to shift this involuntary process and regain the innate power and resilience of our bodies' drive to return to homeostasis, we have to consciously partner with our bodies and teach our brains to recognize what I like to refer to as relative safety.

Relative Safety

Relative safety recognizes that there is no mythological safe place, and healing trauma does not require complete lack of danger. Relative safety means we find safety amidst the danger. This can look like prioritizing having a debrief with friends. It can be looking away from doom scrolling and taking in your actual surroundings. Relative safety can be a moment of silence at a protest, a minute where, as Prentis Hall describes in their IGTV Street Somatics, "if you're out in the streets ... or witnessing on livestream, something you can do to bring your body back down is find something stable. It can be a wall, the floor, just let your body press up against there, find a seat, let your body experience something stable and find your breath (and then) deepen your breath."[1]

There is significant resistance to addressing trauma in our movements. To acknowledge or give time to address trauma seems to be seen as betrayal. For example, how often do we encounter sentiments like, "I'm not going to indulge my feelings about being attacked by police at the protest because it fuels my anger and we all need to be raging like hell to end the police state." This mentality does not serve us. We need to consider building trauma resiliency as an essential and normalized part of our movements and actions. As *Healing in Action: A Toolkit for Black Lives Matter Healing Justice and Direct Action* states:

> In high stakes or high stress situations, we are at greater risk of reacting from a place of trauma. Organizing against violence and for Black liberation can consciously

or unconsciously trigger us to relive unhealed experiences in which we, our ancestors and our communities have been oppressed and violated. That revisited pain becomes the anger that motivates us into action. Yet, sourcing our wounds and trauma in this way takes a hefty toll.[2]

Tools for Building the Power Within

Building trauma resiliency does not have to be a separate thing from the work you are already doing. Once we understand our stress responses as physiological imperatives, we can address them as a necessity. With practice, trauma processing and prevention can become as common sense as bringing a mask and goggles to street actions. And there are many hacks for helping us to integrate trauma resiliency into everyday life.

As a trauma therapist, I help people find ways to listen to the cues of their bodies, and complete the threat response cycles that are repeatedly triggered both on the streets and in daily life. The key to all somatic trauma work is bringing curiosity to how the body is responding in a moment. I bring curiosity to whether a person is hypervigilant, or if their coping mechanism is chronic avoidance. I get curious about their fight/flight/freeze/fawn patterns and how to engage, bring awareness, and shift successfully to complete patterns that are stuck.

In this current moment, one of the recurring things that I see in my office, at protests and other movement spaces is a profound disorientation. COVID-19 has altered our daily lives in disorienting and continually stress-inducing ways. As *Surviving a Pandemic: Tools for Addressing Isolation, Anxiety, and Grief* captures so well: "The fabric of our daily lives was suddenly altered without warning or a clear transition. Along with loved ones who have died or may die in the pandemic, we grieve the loss of the touch of friends, seeing each other's faces."[3]

It is not just the pandemic that leads to our disorientation though, but the trauma we face everyday from living under such a violent and oppressive system, including the utter disregard for Black lives and unapologetic murder of Black people by police. In protests, and demonstrations, this is further intensified by the hyper-violence of the police and white supremacists, which can make it all the more difficult to move away from hyper-vigilance into accurate orienting in these settings.

Restoring the Orienting Response

Whether in the streets or organizing in other spaces, most of us are currently struggling with trauma response in terms of how well we orient. To restore equilibrium, you can begin by simply noticing your pattern. Once you start to notice your own patterned responses, you can then use certain techniques to help better orient. Prentis Hall's advice to sit down or press against a wall is an excellent form of orientation. It uses the sensory system's experience of pressure on the skin and proprioceptive information to orient the body to where you are in time and space.

Additional orientation practices include the following:

Soft scan

This is different from the hypervigilant scan. In the soft scan, you simply allow your head and neck to move slowly, taking in what is life-affirming or pleasurable around you. For example, at a moment of relative calm in a protest, you might slowly scan – not for an escape or to check on your friends – but simply to take in the joy or creativity present, or the love you have for specific friends in the crowd. For this practice, start by scanning in the distance. Allow your eyes to take in what is farthest away. Invite curiosity. This can be done any time outside of protest settings as well. I encourage people to build a practice of orienting or looking around softly whenever entering new environments. It takes less than a minute and helps the nervous system know you are partnering with it for greater resiliency.

Increasing the periphery

Surviving a Pandemic: Tools for Addressing Isolation, Anxiety, and Grief offers this orienting exercise: "Slowly extend your arms out in front of you and move them outward to the edges of what is just within your peripheral view. Once you have found that spot, turn your palms in and slowly wiggle your fingers. As you focus on a point farthest away from you, notice how your eyes soften. Allow your eyes to rest and tap into a deeper sense of centering. Notice how you can hold relaxed vision and pay attention to the movement of your fingers at the same time. In this place, you are in balance with a relaxed alertness, ready to respond to threat from an underlying state of calm."[4]

Responding to Fight and Flight

When our bodies fail to recognize when we no longer need the fight-or-flight response, we get stuck in an endless production of adrenaline. To help the body regain equilibrium, if a person is able to engage the fight/flight muscles even for a moment, this can let the brain know that it is getting the message – i.e., the brain perceives a return to "safety." These simple hacks have given a lot of relief to many people.

Fight and other boundary-protection responses tend to create a lot of physiological activation in the upper body. If you are sitting, you can put the palms of your hands on your thighs or the chair and do a series of push-and-release motions – push for a count of three or longer and then release, really paying attention to the release and lingering on it for a count of three or more. Generally, doing this three times in a row is helpful.

Similarly, flight often lands in our stomach, pelvis, and legs. Sitting down with your feet on the floor, push one foot into the floor and then the other in a slow-motion run. Pay attention to your breath as you do this, and be careful not to force deep breathing, but rather allow your natural breath to come and deepen.

Visualization with Fight and Flight

When returning from stressful or traumatic protests, taking a few minutes to do some visualization can also help to restore the body. If you are having recurring thoughts of a moment when you would have liked to fight or intervene, sit and do the pushing exercise. Then imagine the exact movements you would have acted. Notice the particular muscle systems that would have engaged in order for this to be able to happen. Bring in a fierce ally to do whatever magical thing would need to be done to allow your fight response to be successful, like a magical beast or epic wind gale backing you up as you eviscerate a cop or rescue someone you saw being harmed. The weird thing about somatic work is that when you are attending to your physiological responses, the body does not care whether you are imagining reality or not. When the visualization is done, if you are able, stand up with legs spread comfortably apart, fists on hips and chin up in a power pose, and orient to the present environment and the strength in your body.

For flight visualization, do the slow-motion running exercise while imagining yourself back at the protest, only this time able to turn and run away. Imagine there are plenty of people there to fill your spot, allowing you to turn and leave without any sense of betrayal. Turn your head slightly in both the visualization and in real life, and continue to push your feet – one and then the other – into the floor. Now, imagine the crowd parting for you with care and compassion, allowing you to slowly walk away and onto a magic carpet or bridge that can take you to your relatively safe place, where you are right now. As you are on the magic carpet or bridge, move your neck – again, both in the visualization and in real life – and imagine what you would see on either side of you as you depart the threatening area and enter a path of relative safety. For example, you may picture that you enter a path in a forest between the protests and where you are now.

Return to the Flock

Industrial society, the genocidal violence of white supremacy, and the capitalist idealization of the nuclear family have severed many of us from ritual and community structures necessary for completing stress responses after intense situations. We may not always have a way to surround ourselves with loved ones and "shake it off." Purposeful grounding can be a way to connect deeper and further with our bodies' natural equilibrium, and have that depth of connection buoy and protect you from having intense stress become trauma. The Black Lives Matter *Emotional and Physical Safety in Protest* one-sheet suggests that along with creating a safety and/or support plan, packing a wellness bag and speaking an affirmation can help keep you grounded in purpose (such as Octavia Butler's verse in *Earthseed*: "All that you touch you change / All that you change changes you / The only lasting truth / Is change)."[5]

If you are, in fact, able to return to a group of friends or people who care about you after a protest or stressful situation, try and allow your body to restore equilibrium by shaking it off. This helps to prevent the stress from being stored in the nervous system as trauma, and may look like shivering, laughing, crying, or just resting and letting your body collapse and restore itself.

Debriefing

Covid-19 has robbed us of some of the more natural ways people tend to debrief after protests. We can no longer go to the bar, gather and hug, and see expressions of fear, jubilation, sadness and love mirrored in each other's faces. As a therapist, I hear more stories of people going to protests alone and returning home alone afterward, and then in the aftermath, feeling a profound sense of having to hold all that happened alone. People want me to help them find better coping skills for this isolating period when we don't have access to the same kind of social supports and connections.

Healing in Action: A Toolkit for Black Lives Matter Healing Justice & Direct Action states:

> The time following an action can help lay foundation for the practice of centering healing justice. In trauma research, resilience practices are those which restore us, bringing us back into our motivated and committed selves after a traumatic event. Resilience is distinct from coping. We often use coping strategies to get through or numb out following a trauma. Coping has its own utility, but growth comes from eventually addressing the trauma, initiating healing, and finding resilience.[6]

We need to debrief and create structures of coming together despite the extended nature of the pandemic. The toolkit suggests that debriefs focus not so much on what worked or didn't work, but rather on what feelings are coming up, what was triggered or needs to be healed or repaired in the group, and consciously returning to individual and group purpose.

Collective Care as Resilience

We come to activism and organizing for different reasons – out of hope or anger, alienation or connection, firsthand experience of the damage caused by systems of oppression, or having witnessed that damage with a sense of helplessness and wanting to become empowered to strategically intervene. As anarchists, we want to abolish the world that is built on power over others, and instead create a world where power is held tenderly within each and every one of us and where power is openly shared with each other for the benefit of all.

Building resilience around stress and trauma is not asking us to forgo activism and turn the gaze solely inward; it is simply asking that we use all the tools available to create vibrant and sustainable resistance. Many of us have been trained to view our bodies with disdain. We miss or misunderstand the messages the body sends us. Basic understanding of trauma, the threat response cycle, and how to respond to bodily cues helps us regain an innate strength that is our birthright.

Patrisse Cullors, co-founder of Black Lives Matter, in conversation with Cara Page, a founding member of the Kindred Southern Healing Justice Collective, speaks as someone who has experienced burnout, saying: "I think part of what happens is, as an organizer, especially as a black woman organizer, people think it's 'natural' for us to do the work that we do. That we are exceptional and that this is just what we do there's no care that's needed for us, that there's no care that's given to us in real and thoughtful ways."[7]

It is worth it for each and every one of us, as anarchists, to think critically about how we extend care in various kinds of circumstances, how we receive care, and how and why we resist care. Are you the type of person who extends care by showing up consistently? By checking in on others? By providing or organizing material support? By including members of the group who are outside the main clique? As anarchists, the world we want to build is a caring world, and as the ends cannot justify the means, we must understand that our foundations must be built on care, and that care is different from taking-care-of.

Over the years, I have repeatedly seen groups fracture and implode during times of increased stress, where trauma-induced responses are triggered. Personality differences and strategic preferences that once were tolerable become targets of the trauma induced adrenaline threat response.

It is well documented that stressful events tend to become traumatic when the systems people thought were in place to support them fail, when it feels like no one cares. This is seen in natural (or man-made) disaster recovery work, and currently starkly apparent with the unwillingness of the United States government to effectively respond to the COVID pandemic. Likewise, in grant-funded non-profit movement work, we see people driven to sacrifice their own mental and physical health to meet unsustainable levels of work, under pressure from bosses who cynically place the burden of care onto the individual under the moniker of "self-care." We don't want to replicate these failures.

We need to ask ourselves: What steps can we take to show up for each other with true care, even amongst our differences and our sometimes-conflicting trauma responses and coping strategies? For example, if your response to stress is to move into overdrive – diving into every available activity at full force, and mine is to slow down and look toward developing deeper interpersonal ties – how do we acknowledge and hold these differences tenderly without adapting stances of moral and political superiority? And are we willing to increase self-awareness, deepen our vulnerability, and build resilience within the self as a way to build collective power?

When we trace the biological response to threat in mammals, including humans, we see that the first line of protection, before we turn to fight/flight/freeze, is to simply look for a helper. In the wild, we see young monkeys jump into their mother's arms, deer move closer together at a sign of threat. In my office I see the effects of traumatic events mitigated in people when they have had in their life a caring, grounded adult who was able to be present with them through the trauma, without trying to "fix" it or make it go away.

A simple exercise to practice holding care for one another is as follows:

Sit next to a friend or organizing partner. Acknowledge to yourself that they have everything they need within themselves to heal. Place your hand on their shoulder or firmly press your palm against their upper arm. If no touch is preferred, just sit close together, side by side. First, play with giving too much attention – imagine pushing your helpful intention into them through your hand or look at them with excessive amounts of concern. Then play with being removed. Disconnect your energy so you can hardly feel them through your hand, or hardly notice their presence. Then focus again on just being present with them. Feel your hand on their arm and notice a firm but gentle connection that just says, "I am here." Stay with that and really mark that feeling of presence. Next, take your time and notice their breathing slowly changing the rhythm of your breathing to match theirs. Then slowly deepen your breathing and allow them to deepen their breath in response.

This exercise allows us to explore both what it feels like to give care without being drained, and to accept simple care without avoidance or the need for immediate reciprocation. It builds trust and power on a physiological and interpersonal level. Like the other exercises offered here, it is simple although not always easy, because when we are more able to return to self-regulation and healthy co-regulation, we are also able to more fully experience vulnerability and grief along with flexibility, connection, and joy.

By doing the vulnerable work of identifying stress and trauma responses, deepening our relationships with our physiological cues, and showing up for each other in grounded and sustainable ways, we can break the historical pattern of political movements fracturing, disintegrating, and burning out. By including somatic-based tools in our arsenal, we will be able to build more resilient movements to face the coming years. Ⓐ

Cindy Crabb is a trauma therapist, author, musician, and feminist. Her zine Doris *played a central role in the 1990s girl zine movement associated with third-wave feminism.* Doris *drew attention to sexual assault and consent along with myriad other personal and political topics. She currently resides in Pittsburgh.*

Notes:

1 Prentis Hall teaches with Black Organizing for Leadership and Dignity (https://boldorganizing.org/) and is former Healing Justice Director at Black Lives Matter Global Network (https://blacklivesmatter.com/) and a board member for National Queer and Trans Therapists of Color Network (https://www.nqttcn.com).

2 Black Lives Matter, *Healing in Action: A Toolkit for Black Lives Matter Healing Justice and Direct Action*, October 2017, available at: https://blacklivesmatter.com/wp-content/uploads/2017/10/BLM_HealinginAction-1-1.pdf (accessed on November 24, 2020).

3 CrimethInc., *Surviving a Pandemic: Tools for Addressing Isolation, Anxiety, and Grief*, May 7, 2020, available at: https://crimethinc.com/2020/05/07/surviving-a-pandemic-tools-for-addressing-isolation-anxiety-and-grief (accessed November 24, 2020).

4 Ibid.

5 adrienne maree brown, Autumn Brown, Mark-Anthony Johnson, Naima Penniman, and Adaku Utah, *Emotional and Physical Safety in Protest*, December 18, 2014, available at: https://justhealing.wordpress.com/resourcing-the-work/ (accessed on November 24, 2020).

6 Black Lives Matter, *Healing in Action*.

7 Patrisse Cullors (Co-founder of Black Lives Matter), interview with Cara Page (Founding member of the Kindred Southern Healing Justice Collective), *Good Morning America*. "What is 'Healing Justice'?," aired July 24, 2020, on ABC, https://www.goodmorningamerica.com/culture/video/healing-justice-71932989.

"Michael Reagan's account of class reaffirms for us the centrality of race and gender in the formation of the global working class. Carefully documenting voices of people of color and women in struggle, this book is a work of history in the making, rather than history rendered static in textbooks about Great White Men." —Tithi Bhattacharya

INTERSECTIONAL CLASS STRUGGLE

MICHAEL BEYEA REAGAN

KORIANDRE DAVENPORT, *SHOE SHINE*

JAZZ FRANKLIN, *SHOE CODE*

KARA LYNCH AKA LOVEYBOI AS STAR, *NO TITLE*

ERIN BREE, *CORONASCENE*

CHRIS LIGHT, *I-5 PORTAL*

DISPATCH FROM PORTLAND'S PROTESTS

SARAH MIRK

PERFORMER
CREME BRULEE

I THINK WHAT'S MISSING FROM MEDIA COVERAGE OF THE PROTESTS IS CAPTURING THAT SPIRIT OF JOY. AFTER BEING ISOLATED FOR MONTHS, PEOPLE EXUBERANTLY SHOW UP TO SUPPORT, OFTEN IN GROUPS.

CHEF BLOC!

PEOPLE ARE PROUD TO PROTEST,
TO SAY, "WE'RE HERE."

AT MIDNIGHT, DESPITE THE TEAR GAS, THE DRUM LINE IS STILL GOING STRONG, COMPLETE WITH A TRUMPET AND CONCH SHELL.

Sarah Mirk is a comics journalist, author, and teacher. She works as an editor at The Nib *and as a digital producer for* Reveal. *Her most recent book is* Guantanamo Voices: True Stories from the World's Most Infamous Prison.
www.mirkwork.com

ABOLITION AND THE MOVEMENT
AGAINST POLICE BRUTALITY

THE HEROIC MINNEAPOLIS UPRISING, PROVOKED BY THE PUBLIC lynching of George Floyd, has shaken the entire world. Things that seemed impossible just a couple months ago are now openly discussed and debated at all levels of society.

A prime example is the slogan "Abolish the Police" – which arose with the flames and smoke from the militant protests on Lake Street. "Abolish the Police" was the major, defining slogan of the uprising. It served as a marker of how radical and defiant the movement had become – and how unwilling the young people were to accept the usual kind words and crumbs from the politicians.

The role of police in society should be clear – it is to protect the rich and powerful and preserve the status quo. This is why Black police chiefs, training programs, or civilian oversight have never made a real difference – the underlying purpose of the police is still the same. When you know the history of the police in the United States, from the slave patrols to the deputized thugs that harassed and intimidated the immigrant working class, to today's riot police and assassins – it all starts to makes sense. The Minneapolis Police Department (MPD) is not on our side and never could be. We should focus on building the capacity of working class communities to resist the police and defend our neighborhoods – not tweak the existing repressive apparatus.

The Workers Defense Alliance supports the slogan "Abolish the Police." Our predecessor organization, the General Defense Committee (GDC) – and also our comrades in the former IWW African Peoples Caucus – both raised this slogan in the militant protest movements for Justice for Jamar Clark and Philando Castile more than four years ago.

We promoted abolition as part of our approach of building both militant street resistance to police brutality and organizing "working-class defense groups" to help communities protect themselves from the police and anti-social community violence. For us, the slogan helped explain the role of the police in our society and the folly of trying to reform it into something better. We did not propose "Abolish the Police" as a legislative measure to go lobby liberal politicians, but as the result of the revolutionary struggle of the working-class.

Reformist Abolition?

Since earlier struggles around murders done by police, other abolitionist groups have become more prominent in the Twin Cities. Some of them, like MPD 150, have produced excellent materials detailing the brutal history of the MPD and inviting the community to envision a world without police. New groups like Black Visions Collective and Reclaim the Block have been effectively challenging the power structure to justify any funding of the murderous MPD. But these new abolitionist groups have also pretty much removed revolution from the equation of how to get rid of the police. Instead of preparing the fighting capacity of the working-class and oppressed communities, the focus is on "organizing the politicians" to defund and (maybe) dismantle the police.

The debate around abolishing the MPD now regrettably centers around the strategy of several Minneapolis City Councilors to amend the city charter and take out the provisions that mandate a police department and a minimum number of cops. They say they want to replace the MPD with a new "public safety department" that would emphasize social services, but still retain a smaller number of law enforcement officers. This new agency would be under great pressure to evolve back into the same kind of repressive apparatus the MPD was. If it couldn't do that fast enough, the Hennepin County Sheriff and private security forces would start to fill the gap for the power structure.

Clearly this is not the kind of "abolition" that abolitionists and revolutionaries fight for, even if it does show the power of the uprising to change the debate. Unfortunately, the longer-term community-based and left-wing anti-police brutality groups – all who have made major contributions to the struggle against police murders and violence – are not providing a solid alternative to abolition-lite.

No Alternatives?

The Racial Justice Network, with the NAACP, had a press conference to oppose the charter amendment under the guise of supporting chief Arradondo – the MPD's first Black police chief. They argued that Arradondo had not been given enough time to make changes to the department – and insinuated that the MPD was under attack as a Black-led institution. Nothing could be further from the truth. It has become standard fare for the system to appoint Black chiefs around the country – and nothing ever changes. That's because the system is still the system, and the function of the police is still the function of the police. And while Arradondo is smarter and more charismatic than the local politicians – he is not a good guy. Five people of color have been killed by the MPD during Arradondo's first three years in power – and he attempted to lie about the cause of George Floyd's murder, until the video of his death went viral. People are going to have to decide whether they support the Chief or the people – you can't do both.

Communities United against Police Brutality (CUAPB) has opposed the charter amendment to eliminate the MPD on the grounds that the replacement proposals are poorly written – but this misses the point entirely. Our emphasis should be on doing as much damage to the white supremacist institution of the MPD as possible – not waiting for some perfect replacement from the politicians. CUAPB's alternative to abolition is a long list of reforms to the MPD – some might be better than what we have, and some are downright offensive, like suggesting that cops need more sleep so they'll be less brutal (!). But in either case, this approach ignores the role of the police in our society and tries to return us to a time before the uprising and the popularity of police abolition.

The Twin Cities Coalition for Justice 4 Jamar (which the GDC used to participate in several years ago) actually organized a lobby campaign to stop the city charter from being amended, thus maintaining the status quo for the MPD (!). They have dressed up this betrayal of the uprising by arguing that the City Council can't be trusted, that police can't be abolished under capitalism, and that what's really needed is so-called "community control" of the MPD. This is a thoroughly dishonest and sectarian argument. Of course the City Council can't be trusted – but that doesn't mean that the government won't sometimes concede to popular pressure. For instance, the City Council previously passed a watered-down minimum wage increase in response to the Fight for $15 campaign. Should we have lobbied the City Council not to pass the wage increase because it didn't go far enough? But the coalition's alternative is actually more conservative than the City Council's plan. The coalition proposes a Civilian Police Accountability Council (CPAC), modeled after a campaign in Chicago. This campaign's strategy is to get support from the City Council and/or amend the city charter – the exact same approach they hypocritically criticize when it comes to defund/disband efforts. There was no sentiment in the uprising for "community control" of the police – people know that the various attempts at civilian oversight have all been frauds. CPAC supporters argue this would be different because it would have an elected board. But why would this board have any more of a radical character than the City Council elected by the same voters?

If it's utopian to think the police can be abolished under capitalism, its equally naive to think the community can exercise "control" over the murderous MPD.

CPAC does not get rid of the police or even cut the police department budget. Instead it creates a big new city government bureaucracy that will supposedly hold the police accountable to the community. But if it's utopian to think the police can be abolished under capitalism, it's equally naive to think the community can exercise "control" over the murderous MPD. Any CPAC bureaucracy with its middle-class staff, attorneys, investigators, and other specialists would actually have a material interest in the continuation of the MPD – not it's abolition.

Our Approach

So what should our approach be to the City Council's maneuvers? First we should avoid getting bogged down in the lobbying at city hall. These efforts are designed to pull activists off the street and into the logic of system-politics. It was the uprising that put this discussion on the table, not the politicians. Let's keep our focus on the communities and class that carried out the rebellion. Second, we should aggressively promote the concept of abolition of the police – not in a watered-down, reformist way, but in a clearly argued revolutionary framework that includes building up working-class defense organizations and expropriating needed resources from the rich. We should expose attempts to label things "abolition" that are clearly not. We should also get better at discussing and debating the real questions, concerns, and criticisms many people have about abolition of the police. Third, and most importantly, we must push ahead with the building up of working-class defense organizations and other autonomous forms of working-class power. Ⓐ

Reprinted with permission from The Defender: 'zine of the Twin Cities Workers Defense Alliance *(Twin Cities, Fall 2020)*

A VOICE FROM MINNEAPOLIS'S GEORGE FLOYD SQUARE

*This interview was conducted
in the summer of 2020.*

Could you say a little bit about who you are and your background?

Marcia: I have lived and taught in South Minneapolis for the last twenty-two years. Before I was an English teacher, I was a non-commissioned officer in the Marines.

How did the murder of George Floyd hit you, personally?

My house is 260 steps from Cup Foods, door to door. I can go and pick up an item while still having food on the burner. I can see that corner from my sunroom window. The morning after his murder, I realized that a girl I taught had filmed it, and my concern for her melded with my outrage about the murder of this Black man. The callousness of our society toward Black lives and Black psyches has been demonstrated on that corner time and time again. It's terrorism.

Can you describe how the George Floyd Square Memorial "autonomous zone" came to be – and your role in it?

When the protestors flooded the square, my contribution was simply to hand out masks because of the threat of the coronavirus. Then, I appointed myself chief of parking on my block because wave after wave of mourners and protestors continued to arrive. By the time I realized that many were not leaving, I saw the shift of that intersection from a rally point, to a fortified place of resistance. The protestors occupied the space, standing in solidarity, day and night, despite gas attacks and rubber bullets and the National Guard rolling in. I realized that the people had laid claim to this piece of Minneapolis and would not surrender it.

It was when the ad hoc barricades were fortified with concrete ones, that I knew we were in it for the long haul. That was when the mutual aid, communal meals, field medic stations, and the band of security all made up the city of Floyd Town, the autonomous zone. The police were told they weren't welcome, the phrase "F12" written on every conceivable surface. But other services were denied us as well.

In the first days of the uprising, we did not even have mail service. It truly felt like we'd been cut off from the city. However, we negotiated trash pickup and sanitation services, then set about keeping the barricades place safe, secure, and sacred.

Why has this memorial space been so important?
How has it functioned in relation to the broader uprising?

This memorial space has been held as a place of protest and a place of pride in the solidarity of the diverse group of people standing up for Black, brown, and Indigenous people. People have made pilgrimages from all over the world to this site to see the flash point for a global reckoning with inequity and state brutality.

You see even the most casual tourist experience Mari Hernandez's Street of Names and openly weep for the unavenged dead. This site has symbolic power. It is already a national historic site because the nation has made it so.

How have the police treated the space?

The police have played a sly propaganda game. They have played up to the press the idea of "hostile crowds" preventing them from entering either the barricaded area or surrounding streets in order to justify a work slow-down and refusal of services to the predominantly white citizens in the surrounding thirties blocks. This attempt to gin up resentment and a backlash to the movement has been further aided by a deliberate, concerted effort by people told to shoot fireworks and rounds into the air for weeks on end to set off the shot spotter and flood the precinct with calls. It might as well been called "Operation: How ya like them apples?" The irony is that the police have a near-constant presence with plainclothes officers and aerial drone cameras. They also circle the surrounding blocks all day, yet refuse to respond to 911 calls from the harried citizens who still reach for the phone at every sound of gunfire. It's an op. Plain and simple.

What have you been most proud of and encouraged by? And what have been the biggest problems or challenges in George Floyd Square?

I have been really encouraged by the diversity of the protestors who gather to protest police brutality. That so many people are putting their bodies on the line to stand in solidarity with the marginalized folks in this country. I'm proud to see signs that acknowledge missing, exploited, and ignored Indigenous women. I cried when a brother held a sign that said, "If we ain't for trans Black people, we ain't for Black people." I am overwhelmed daily by the momentum. It is there. Even in the quiet of the square, there may be a march of thousands in downtown or hundreds in a suburb. We are serious about this liberation.

Yet, in the microcosm of this Autonomous Zone, I see the fine working of capitalism and blunt instrument of the violence that it can wield in the form of gunfire. This prevailing narrative of lawlessness and danger had been orchestrated with the cooperation of the powers-that-be-and-always-been in the 30s blocks of South Minneapolis. We have sat and watched them all work seamlessly to get the desired effect: a return to status quo. It would be actually admirable if it weren't so tragic. It's like watching *Birth of a Nation* in real life.

You've described yourself as an abolitionist. How has this experience informed your views?

Considering the overt, covert, and tacit cooperation of the police with folks that they will eventually indict, I say: throw it all out and start fresh. We have to remake and reimagine what our social services (including apprehension) look and feel and function like. I cannot believe we cannot do it.

But it must be dismantled as it stands now. This belief solidified itself after sixty-three days in the zone, when I'd been a tepid reformist at the beginning.

What do you think is coming next for this movement in Minneapolis?

The next step is picking up the gauntlet again. The city should be wincing in anticipation of the slap, the challenge, the calling out, and the showing up. If I have to take a Sawsall and take the Thirty-Eighth and Chicago sign to our next place of occupation, our next protest site, I will. This is just the beginning. Ⓐ

Reprinted with permission from The Defender: 'zine of the Workers Defense Alliance *(Twin Cities, Fall, 2020)*

CAN YOU HEAR ME NOW?

VERENA SCHÄFERS SUTHERLAND

"HELLO AHMED, CAN YOU HEAR ME?" I HALF-SHOUT INTO MY LAPTOP, which is precariously balanced on two couch cushions. Our geriatric mutt, Tucker, is gently snoring in the background, only his two grizzled ears visible against the red and black blanket. I see Ahmed, a mustachioed elderly man with kind eyes, through the ubiquitous Zoom app, looking down at what I presume to be his phone, waving at me, smiling, but no sound comes. Well, fuck. I take a look at the participant list in our conference call, which happens to include just the two of us and happens to also reveal the answer: Ahmed does not have his audio connected.

Ahmed, one of the seven beginning-level students in my English to Speakers of Other Languages (ESOL) Level 2 class at the local community college has suddenly been pushed into an online learning modality that I, a veteran teacher of ESOL for fifteen years but now robbed of many of the skills I was so fluently able to apply in the classroom, find similarly confounding. Being an older man from Iraq, he finds the technology aspect of this new reality daunting. He has a laptop, he says, but he doesn't know how to use it. I ask him to show it to me over Zoom. The screen remains a matte black, no matter which button he pushes. I suspect it may be out of battery power and ask him if he would like to speak to a translator about this. He shakes his head, no. Definitely not. It hurts his pride that I asked.

Ahmed is one of seven beginning-level English learners braving this sudden onset of online learning together with me, and it feels like we are all making it up as we go along. As always, my group of students is diverse. No one-size approach will fit these individuals.

There is Nadya, who is very shy on our first call, but extremely studious. She prefers written feedback, and asks her questions via email. Gmail, Zoom, WhatsApp, Google Drive, YouTube videos – you name it, she can navigate it all. She doesn't know what the "be" verb is, but she can run circles around me technologically. Over the course of the term, I meet George, her young son. When we study, she keeps him busy with movies, or on WhatsApp calls with her family in Belarus. He is shy about the camera but shows me his *Paw Patrol* watch in my second office hour. Nadya is the only student who joins me regularly for conversation practice, and she now smiles more during our conversations, whereas before she would frown in concentration. I know she is one of the lucky ones. She is going to be ok – the be-verb will come.

Besa, from the Kosovo, finds this world harder to exist in. When talking to me becomes overwhelming for her, she puts her husband on the line. On our third call, both the husband and I are feeling frustrated. I can tell that I'm no longer being as kind and patient as I think of myself as being. We're all stretched thin. I ask to talk to Besa again. I show her the "be" verb again. *Damn the "be" verb,* I think. I just made a YouTube video about it. But she does show up to our online classes, and she assures me she's learning. The words of our department chair echo in my mind: engagement over content. I'm beginning to understand what she means.

Being deaf and visually impaired, remote learning comes with a very different set of challenges for Fenglian, who arrives with a team of four amazing American Sign Language (ASL) interpreters who quietly attend our Zoom calls, signing to Fenglian what I and the other students are discussing. During group work times, when the others are in breakout rooms, I chat with Fenglian.

"Everything ok?" I type. She signals "yes," her hand a fist rocking back and forth on the screen. She taught me that this means "yes," right after she taught me how to sign her guide dog's name, Cruzer. I know that Cruzer loves to chase balls.

These students are my success stories. It's not easy teaching them, and I often feel lost. But I also feel free. I can make things up as I go along. Nobody is telling me to be in a classroom at a certain time. There are no rules about which learning modalities I need to use. A sense of freedom and chaos prevails as I recklessly photograph pages from the copyrighted book and put them online. The library is closed, after all, and how else would I make books accessible to those students of mine who can't afford to buy one? While that is a positive aspect of this new way of teaching, the inequality of the system is put into sharp focus for me as well. Our department chair is scrambling to devise a system that allows students access to Chromebooks for the duration of the term, but it is not finished when the start of the term rolls around. Toward the end of the term, I find out that I could have ordered a Chromebook for students that need one. How did I miss that memo? A quick peek at my 526 unread emails tells me that it wasn't the only memo I missed.

My initial thirteen enrolled students quickly dwindle to seven, and it becomes clear to me: this is a supply problem. An email crosses my feed: a hard-fighting Level 3 teacher asking again about those Chromebooks for her students. It sounds like they never arrived. I'm suddenly feeling extremely ineffective, and even more tired. During a normal term in a Level 2 class, I struggle to support students who lack basic literacy while balancing them with those who already have academic degrees, without causing frustration to either party. Of course, this is my desire, but it is at the best of times nothing but a pretty story I tell myself. I know both ends of the spectrum are frustrated, and I'm aiming for an imaginary middle, often knowing I'm missing the mark.

While these realities of ESOL are acknowledged in department meetings and conversations between tired evening teachers, not much is done about them. We are told that we are doing the best we can, but is the college doing the best *it* can? The already impossible-to-bridge chasm has now widened considerably and suddenly includes technology access and user skills – an issue that had thus far been reserved for Levels 6 to 8. Not only are those less tech-savvy left behind, they are not even given the opportunity to show up.

All of us teachers know and have discussed openly that some students would not be able to participate. Nala, a student with a scholarship and full institutional support, received a Chromebook, but her family has no Internet. She is signed up for class, and the scholarship has paid her tuition, but now her advisor tells me she (the advisor) is considering buying a Comcast account for the family. I don't hear back from the advisor for a week, and Nala herself is too flustered even to answer a text message from me. She never does join my class. I have no idea if she now has Internet access. She is not alone in her struggle. Many of my students use the expensive data on their phones to connect to class on small phone screens initially, and then decide it's not worth it. I share my screen during our meetings, knowing full well that not everyone is able to see what I'm typing. I want there to be a better way, so I post notes and record meetings. I dream of a world where free universal Wi-Fi is the norm, a world where pleas for Chromebooks don't go unanswered.

This is my desire, but it is at the best of times nothing but a pretty story I tell myself.

So many are dropping out. The seven left standing become four. Each of the four students has access to two things: Internet at home and a laptop. Where does this leave people who don't have these resources? What could I have done to support them? While I try hard not to lay blame on myself, some do feel like personal failures on my part. Like Maria. When we had our first full class meeting, she had attempted to use an outdated Zoom link to connect to the class. While I was having a blast, talking with the students together as a group for the first time, doing what I do so well, sort of, Maria was desperately messaging me through every channel available to her, stuck outside our little Zoom room. She later texted me saying, "I don't know if this will work for me." I thought, same, Maria, same. A few days later she had dropped the class. I talked to my department chair about this during a meeting. After an abortive attempt to joke about this – yes, this is what is has come to, she smiles sadly and says, "We can't keep them all." I nod and think, *But we should try harder. I should try harder.* I truly think that, and at the same time I know that nobody is paying me for this emotional labor – or all the extra work of putting materials online.

On the other hand, I am truly impressed with the support the college provides through disabilities services. Fenglian is a Chinese student who has severe visual impairment in addition to her being deaf. Her first language is ASL. The initial interview with Fenglian is a ninety-minute ordeal of missed connections and attempts to make this situation workable for her, her interpreters, and for me. In the end, we reach a point where Fenglian can read what I share, see the ASL interpreters, and can kind of see me. It's the best we can do.

One time, one of the ASL interpreter's kids runs around on screen, just as I return from breaking up a fight between our resident shepherd and my fearless tuxedo cat. Kids running on screen, mothers – always mothers – scrambling to contain them while maintaining a smooth, professional facade. I see it crack, sometimes, that facade. Someone tiredly eating a breakfast bagel and sipping coffee at 10 a.m. during class. A quick reach for the mute button a few seconds too late to conceal the noisy fight between siblings. Nadya shouting something in Russian over her shoulder and then turning back to the camera, a slight embarrassed smile on her face, saying, "Sorry, just one minute." We all smile in solidarity: this is our life now; this is what it looks like.

But I'm feeling ok, I think. I'm fine. This is fine. I can do this. Never mind the overwhelmed, worries about my family in Germany (though they are probably and rightfully more worried about me), technological glitches, and desperate messages from my department chair. Never mind that I was given this class four days before it started, and I didn't want it, but I had to take it because – money. I should be grateful to have a job; isn't that how it works? It's not supposed to be this way. Never mind that there is a revolution going on, and everyone is strained and stretched thin.

The department tries to support us in this time. Full time employees are tasked with drumming up resources, which result in offerings such as weekly Zoom support groups (on Zoom of course), an avalanche of Google Docs with teaching ideas and links to helpful sites, and even a virtual cocktail hour. While I don't participate much, I at least feel an effort has been made to help us teach. We are being thanked at least on a weekly basis. Look at all those teachers scrambling. "You all are amazing" is the catch phrase. Somewhere in there I can't shake the feeling that educators, students, and administrators alike are being asked to handle an almost impossible situation with very few resources, though.

That is, when I give myself time to feel and process. I feel like I'm in survival mode all the time now. I'm trying hard to keep up with the many messages from administration coming my way that seem to amount to us teachers being told to hold it down and make it up as best we can. In week four I pretty much stop checking my emails. I know our department chair will text me if I miss something important, an act of kindness I'm deeply grateful for. When I look again in week eleven I see that I missed something, sure, but there is so much noise. How can we filter the noise?

Taking attendance has been up to my discretion this term too. I look at the shared Google doc and put in three hours for Monday for everyone who submitted their homework, no matter whether they checked in with me or not. I can make this choice on my own, I have it in black-on-white pixels on my email screen, one of the twenty-five tabs currently open in my browser as I try to simultaneously record a YouTube video, add the correct hyperlink to my WebEasy page, that lowest of high-tech options the college offers, organize the folder with audio files for listening activities, and keep my cat from puking on the sofa. Of course, two hours later I receive a text message from a student telling me I linked to the wrong page in the book. I apologize and fix it. And

I feel like I'm in survival mode all the time now.

then I realize – I'm late entering attendance again. Usually, I would have an email about this now, or a text. But nothing. Silence. I realize I am not the only one who is overwhelmed.

I am, of course, not at all the only teacher going through fatigue at this time. My fellow Level 2 teacher Sue and I half-heartedly exchange phone numbers, try for a Zoom meeting a couple of times, tell ourselves we really should be reaching out, until we give up. We tell each other there is no need to reinvent the wheel. Let's just share materials. A great idea in theory, but in practice even just creating a shared Google folder and annotating documents to make them usable for someone else seems overwhelming. In the end, I just send her to my WebEasy page and tell her it's all there. I have no idea if she looks at it. I know others are much more successful in their efforts to share the load, and toward the end of the term, I finally feel like next term, I might be up for a more collaborative effort. But I do not get a class for summer term, which does not come as a huge surprise.

I wonder what's wrong with me that I struggle so much to connect at the moment, and then I realize that it is because the effort to do so is put on the teachers' shoulders. I'm feeling pretty numb. But I do feel alive when things go well, when I feel like I'm actually teaching. My partner, now suddenly privy to my teaching, says (is that awe in his voice?), "I think you're a really good teacher. There was definitely learning going on." Somehow, this brings tears to my eyes. There are so many threads, so many individual stories. I struggle to gauge if learning is going on. But the final exam, posted on Google Docs and proctored through my laptop camera and, of course, Zoom, shows me: there is. On some level,

I have been able to get through more materials and cover more ground than ever before. On another level, I know this is because the students self-selected, which means I have reached far fewer people.

"Okay, Ahmed, can you hear me now?" I say, well-knowing that he can't. The Zoom app clearly shows that his cell phone audio is not connected. In an abortive attempt to fix the issue, I accidentally kick him out of the call. I hold my breath and swear. I'm swearing a lot these days. Quickly, I open tab twenty-six in my browser, Google Voice, to text him, "I'm so sorry. Click this link to speak to me." Will I ever see Ahmed again? Is he going to drop the class as well? Just a few minutes later, he is back, smile turned to frown, but without sound. A sudden brainstorm has me waving my own phone at the camera. He nods. I'm not sure what we're saying, but we're communicating. I connect my own phone to the Zoom call, which causes a terrible screeching in the system, but fortunately my student can't hear it. He looks a bit confused because he can see me double on his screen. I hold the phone up to the camera, very close, and show him where to turn on the sound. He shrugs, looking mildly desperate now. It's not working. I click through some settings. Oh. There. "Disconnect audio," it says. That seems like a very reasonable button to click when audio is the only thing you understand. I click the button. I show Ahmed my phone again. He nods, with me now. I show him how to reconnect the audio. I smile, then I show him again. I smile, and I wait. About a minute later, Ahmed's face crunched up into a focused frown, I hear a crackling on my computer.

"Hello, can you hear me?" I say, again, as if that's the only thing I can say anymore.

"Yes, I can hear you, teacher," Ahmed says. We both smile. After we hang up, I know, I hope, I think that Ahmed can do this online education thing – another success story. Until he drops out in week eight. Ⓐ

Verena *is an animal trainer as well as a recovering teacher from Portland, Oregon. When she's not outdoors with dogs or horses, she spends her time learning punk classics on the ukulele, exploring fantastical realms of all sorts both in books and through role-playing games groups and snuggling up with one of her many pets.*

All names have been changed to protect the privacy and identities of students.

IS ANOTHER WORLD POSSIBLE?
PANDEMIC COMMUNALISM AS A CURE TO CORONA CAPITALISM

JEAN DESTA

AS MILLIONS OF PEOPLE AROUND THE GLOBE WENT INTO ISOLATION, WE started asking ourselves how we should react to this situation. Many felt the need to go and help, while others blindly followed the guidelines and restrictions imposed by governments. At the same time, the system's contradictions – even during an enormous public health crisis – emerged ever more clearly. As these types of calamities are happening more frequently, this is becoming our new reality. And it is increasingly clear that there is a need to find an alternative that puts people and nature back at the center of politics.

When a society is confronted with an unexpected catastrophe, be it warlike conflict, a sudden scarcity of resources, or a natural phenomenon, human empathy, mutual aid, and solidarity tend to come to the fore. Despite the ideological dominance of capitalism, humans still possess an almost reflexive tendency to come together and develop spontaneous forms of support and collective organization, even during times of deep agony. Humans are fundamentally social animals. Coming together is also a means for her to deal with stress, uncertainty, and insecurity in a changing environment. This trend has happened so often and in such different circumstances that it has been granted its own name: "disaster communism."[1]

For centuries, liberals and other preachers of the state system persuaded people through psychological, social scientific, and philosophical theories to believe that humans need to be under centralist control to prevent falling into a state of perennial war against each other. According to these theories, in the case of disaster, citizens would only think for themselves, selfishly looting and preying on others. The whole of "official history" has been written to support these perspectives, most of which have their roots in Thomas Hobbes's ideas about the "state of nature." In Hobbesian speculations, statelessness equals a so-called "state of nature" in which "man is a wolf to man" and "a war of all against all" mentality would prevail. In this way, statehood, centralization, and institutionalized hierarchies are rationalized.

Nevertheless, since the seventeenth century, political philosophers and social movements have contested Hobbesian theory and the liberal paradigm. In the nineteenth century, Karl Marx, Mikhail Bakunin, and Peter Kropotkin, among other leading socialist theorists of the emergent workers' movement, argued for a more social, empathic, and communal view of humanity. In his book *Mutual Aid: A Factor of Evolution* Kropotkin, for example, countered the social Darwinism that was prevalent at that time. Kropotkin advanced a view that mutual aid and cooperation determine the natural world, including survival of species and evolution, as much as competition between individuals. These ideas have been developed further in the twentieth century and reinforced with the methodology of new social sciences, particularly anthropology and sociology.

Within the discipline of anthropology, researchers such as Pierre Clastres and Eduardo Viveiros de Castro have written about communities that are not only stateless but have also organized themselves into communal structures that actively prevent the emergence and formation of centralized state. Anthropologist researchers David Graeber and James C. Scott observe that many stateless societies have actually been based on communal values of sharing and reciprocity and haven't remotely resembled Hobbesian ideas of the "state of nature." In fact, Graeber and Scott agree that those communities have steadfastly adhered to their communal lifestyle and actively resisted the emergence of state, centralization, and class society.

In his book *Debt: The First 5,000 Years*, Graeber argues that these communal values and practices live in the people's consciousness and praxis even long after state formation. As he explains, this "everyday communism" forms the basis for all human sociability even in capitalist societies. According to Graeber, the existence of capitalism is dependent on a vast amount of everyday interactions that follow distinctively communistic ethics of sharing and reciprocity instead of the liberal market logic of individual benefit and exchange value. As most of everyday social interactions fall in this category, society should be recognized as independent from state and capital. Similar analyses have been put forward by Murray Bookchin in his book *The Ecology of Freedom* and Abdullah Öcalan, who attracted global attention with his five-volume book *Manifesto for a Democratic Civilization*.

Applying the research of the above referred theorists to the question, disaster communism must be viewed as liberation, intensification, and expansion of the communal and communistic practices of society in a situation where unexpected disruption (natural or human-generated catastrophe) loosens the pressure of liberalism, the state, and capitalism.

Having researched human response to earthquakes, wildfires, explosions, terror attacks, and hurricanes in the twentieth century, in her book *A Paradise Built in Hell* Rebecca Solnit also argues that practical evidence

"No to blackmail between health and wages."

PHOTO BY CAMILLA BIANCHI, BRIGADE GERDA TARO

supports the communal view on human organizing rather the Hobbesian constructions. According to Solnit, in situations where the state suddenly becomes dysfunctional, or where statist and capitalist governance breaks down, humans show more solidarity and responsibility toward other humans and the environment, not less.

Epidemics, however, are a catastrophe of a unique nature. They force us to reevaluate not only our understanding of ourselves, human relationships and our societies, but also our comprehension of crisis behavior and organization. Epidemics disrupt not only the material but also the social basis of a community. Indeed, epidemics seem to be the most antisocial of all crises, striking directly against our social and communal character while exacerbating inequality within society. Because of the coronavirus, people in several countries cannot even mourn their loved ones together. For months funerals have been forbidden and family and friends of the deceased have had to grieve alone.

Going Beyond the Crises: Pandemic Communalism

The coronavirus has brought huge disruptions to everyday life, social relations, and most importantly, conventional ways of mobilizing political and humanitarian initiatives. It is clear that COVID-19 is just a symptom of a much larger and systemic problem that points to the capitalist system and its domination of nature. Climate change and its effects will be more and more present in our lives if states do not change course and try to reduce carbon emissions effectively.

As we navigate this new pandemic world, it is clear that human behavior resulting in disaster communism will not emerge spontaneously on a scale sufficient to face epidemic crises. Yet, a lack of meaningful and communal participation may have enormous humanitarian, psychological, and societal consequences given the need to go beyond the material concerns and to provide answers to our socio-emotional and even spiritual needs in times of agony. Epidemics affect every aspect of society; therefore, disaster relief and solutions must also reflect all of society holistically. Instead of the often spontaneous and local disaster communism, we may call this approach "pandemic communalism" to highlight its organized, societal, and federal nature.

The term "communalism" originated in the Paris Commune of 1871, when Parisians took up arms to defend a confederation of cities and towns they had created as an alternative to the republican nation-state. It has gained currency more recently in the writings of Murray Bookchin, who describes it as an assembly form of grassroots democracy in which autonomous confederated municipalities collaborate in creating a powerful political and economic network that stands in opposition to the nation-state.

Pandemic communalism should be the inspiration that gives a concrete political and organizational framework for organizing a society that is facing pandemic disaster. In fact, we should use this moment as an opportunity to transcend the limits imposed by the established system and to bring politics back to the

COVID-19 is just a symptom of a much larger and systemic problem that points to the capitalist system and its domination of nature.

center of community life, thereby regaining its original meaning as the self-administration of a community. The perspective of pandemic communalism aims to establish new institutions outside the state, built within and around communities wherever there is a void left by governments unable to understand and to meet the real needs of communities in time of a disaster. Moreover, pandemic communalism challenges the current system by offering answers that are outside the state framework, empowering communities to advance their own organizational capabilities. In order to pursue this path, there is need for a high degree of commitment, responsibility, and creativity.

In the past few months there have been several movements around the world trying to tackle issues that the pandemic has aggravated. Doctors went to the streets of California to take care of homeless patients. Housing activists called for rent strikes.[2] From Spain to the United States, more and more people (up to one-third of households just in the US)[3] have not been able or willing to pay their rent. Other solidarity campaigns and actions have started around the globe, with a varying degree of organization as each country and movement has tried to face the crisis in different ways. Pandemic communalism simply means a federative umbrella under which all such initiatives become an organized social power and reclaim a continuously widening part of social life through popular self-administration.

In Milan, Italy, as soon as the outbreak hit the city, "solidarity brigades" were established. In the course of two months almost 1,000 people joined the brigades to support others and almost fourteen brigades started operating in the city. These brigades helped elderly people who were advised not to leave the house with their grocery shopping and medicines and supplied people who lost their jobs with food. And another brigade was established to provide psychological support to anyone struggling emotionally during this time of isolation and hardships.

As the brigades started working, it was clear there was a need to approach the crisis in a very different way from the past. Valerio, one of

the representatives of the Milanese Solidarity Brigades, explained that "everything needed to be re-evaluated" and a certain amount of discipline established in relation to hygienic measures, performance of tasks and other routines.[4] Milan set an example and soon the brigades spread well beyond Italy.[5] Similar groups formed in France, Spain, the United States, and Brussels. At the moment there are fifty-four brigades around the world. "We are talking to one another and sharing experiences and perspectives," said Clara, who is working in the coordination group for the Milanese brigades. As the pandemic appears to come under greater control, most of the countries are lifting some of the very restrictive measures, and most of the brigades are asking themselves what will be next and how they should approach the so-called "Phase 2."

Unlike conventional forms of organization that have emerged in past crises, pandemic communalism is not born from semi-spontaneous networks that develop in mass meetings, protests and gatherings. In this crisis, the starting point is extreme physical isolation. During epidemics, it is organization, trust, and discipline that allow larger and larger gatherings, not the other way around. The first mission in constructing pandemic communalism is, therefore, to develop a form of organization of mutual aid that can break the isolation and bring people together.

Fundamental for pandemic communalism is a mentality that each and every human can have a positive influence on the wellbeing of people in their environment. So far, the state mentality has pushed a single narrative: everyone is a potential virus carrier, so it is better to stay home, isolated, and if anyone dares to step out of their homes, he or she is singled out and accused of not caring for their own community. Meanwhile, thousands of non-essential factories and industries have continued working, and effectively continued as the hubs of contagion. Most of the time workers were not provided with the right protective equipment. In so doing, the state's intent is to blame citizens while failing to recognize its own responsibilities in the crises.

This view that salaried work is the only legitimate way to participate in society is severely limited. There are multiple other ways to be active and to contribute to the good of society by voluntary and self-organized means. Even rudimentary collective structures can protect people belonging to risk groups. Groceries have often been cited as a simple and concrete example: if neighbors divide shopping in shifts, they can have foodstuffs with minimal close contacts. Such division and rotation of tasks and responsibilities can be established for most everyday needs. Thus, human contacts and the epidemic growth speed can be decreased while simultaneously building community organization.

The main characteristic of pandemic communalism is to expand primarily in the field of reproductive labor – all forms of labor that reproduce the workforce, and the material and social basis of production. Child bearing, education, health care, cleaning, cooking and other housework as well as different forms of care work are often cited as examples of reproductive labor. Studying can also be seen as reproductive work when people prepare and educate themselves for what the system calls "real" or productive work. In capitalist societies reproductive labor is performed mainly by women, whether it be in non-salaried work at home or wage labor. Therefore, it has become a field of analysis, critique, and resistance for revolutionary feminists such as Silvia Federici and Selma James.

Housing, education, upbringing, child care, and care work in general as well as feeding are precisely the basic questions to which the pandemic communalism perspective attempts to provide new solutions that are not based on the state or patriarchal family. Pandemic communalism is, therefore, oriented toward feminism and women's liberation. Communal structures have the possibility – and even the duty – to overcome traditional gender roles and the resulting barriers and division of work. The problems of households are also not limited to the questions of economy and sustainability, but to problems such as alcoholism and substance abuse, domestic violence, and mental health issues that are central in times of quarantine. Solutions for these issues must be formulated and provided.

First Steps Toward Pandemic Communalism

There is no need to be an organized group to start working toward pandemic communalism. Depending on the neighborhood, an apartment building, or even a tiny group of smaller houses, could be the context in which to start organizing relevant responsibilities, roles, and tasks. A community of some dozens of people should be enough to take care of most basic everyday needs. These needs could include, for example: helping people running errands (groceries, post office, library, pharmacy); sharing responsibility for children in case schools are shut down; making the Internet, cars, common spaces, and other basic resources available for common use; even purchasing and distributing prime necessities collectively should they become scarce in the future.

When apartment complexes, or whole neighborhoods, become organized, the primary question is then how can they coordinate with other similar units. Committees or working groups for autonomous health care, food supply, domestic problems, and other logistics can be established to confront issues that are common for all. Each region, city, and neighborhood will organize itself as defined by its own characteristics, depending on the level of social organization prior to the epidemic and other factors. In some cities there are plenty of existing mutual aid groups, neighborhood organizations, and other groups whose role is boosted in these times. Other cities and neighborhoods have started to organize themselves virtually from scratch, from the informal connections and ties between the inhabitants. However, every locality faces the same questions: How to take over more responsibilities and expand the functioning of these self-administered structures and networks? How to unify all the different initiatives into an organized and coordinated entity? How to build social power beyond reciprocal mutual aid with limited resources? These are the main questions that arise when initiatives start to federate their activities and structures, bringing to life the societal and confederal perspective of pandemic communalism. At this point, pandemic communalism transcends the limits of single relief efforts and starts to take shape as an alternative communal fabric of everyday life and to reveal its systemic character.

In the time of an epidemic, social self-organization should be based on the principles of decentralization and compartmentalization. Compartmentalization means dividing a crowd of people into small "compartments" and minimizing close contact between the different compartments. Such organization is developed to prevent the spread of sickness to other units and to protect the whole, if one of them is contaminated. The state's curfew policy is using the same logic, trying to control movements – and thus contagion – between different districts, cities, and even neighborhoods.

However, if state-imposed compartmentalization and isolation is fully implemented it will destroy the decision-making structures, production, and societal logistic and thus, at the end of the day, the whole society. The compartmentalization of a city, for example, is practically limited by the fact that people

Pandemic communalism transcends the limits of single relief efforts and starts to take shape as an alternative communal fabric of everyday life.

tend to not work in the area where they live (not even in the same city sometimes), that local groceries cannot feed the people of the neighborhood, and on the neighborhood level there are no decision-making structures that would guarantee the continuation of social life.

Rigid centralized governments and companies that follow the irrational logic of markets with their grocery stores and miles-long supply chains are thus becoming obstacles to the counter-epidemic policies. The ability to adapt to new circumstances and resilience can be increased with a combination of decentralization and coordination, i.e., with more local democracy and federalism. This is the true meaning of pandemic communalism. Local democratic structures increase people's capability to make decisions about their lives and react to emerging material problems rapidly and therefore empower the society – regardless of whether any epidemic and mass quarantine are in place or not.

The Political Perspective

A natural foundation of social crisis organizing is mitigation of the humanitarian consequences of a crisis with self-organization and mobilization of local communities and their resources. It differs from the state approach in that social organizing doesn't only seek to heal the symptoms, but also to empower local communities and, as a result, the whole society. With the creation of locally rooted and self-governed structures of decision-making, security, care, and logistics, a society shall be not only "restored" but transformed. From the perspective of pandemic communalism it is not enough to seek to return to the pre-crisis state, but to construct solutions that will not result in yet another crisis, whether economic or environmental in nature.

At the same time, the economic repercussions of the coronavirus pandemic and its countermeasures are just beginning to be understood. It is clear already that we are entering a new economic crisis; only its magnitude is uncertain. Many analysts are talking about a global recession that might reshape the economic sector for a long time. In the first weeks of the coronavirus outbreak, financial markets around the world sank, while investors and banks were hoping for a quick fix. Production stopped, and so did consumption. We have seen a severe rise in unemployment, and the economic crisis is far deeper than the stock markets indicate. Economists are warning that there is a historically wide gap between the indicators of the real economy and the expectations of stock markets.[6] It is a superficial result of the cheap money that central banks pumped into markets very rapidly in the beginning of the pandemic. However, we should not delude ourselves that the system will collapse by itself with no viable alternative. After all, capitalism is the most dynamic system of all time, and therefore it will try to adapt to this crisis and move on. COVID-19 has already shown us how certain corporations, such as Amazon, took advantage and made large profits while forcing their workers to operate without adequate protective gear.[7]

While unemployment, inequality, and difficulties to pay rent and other bills increase, and institutional social security becomes overwhelmed, material problems will reach a level that require organized and broad forms of collective action. Material support can be organized up to a point with the more or less informal networks of friends, relatives, and neighbors. Housing, electricity, water, and other fundamental needs, on the other hand, cannot be guaranteed with the deeds of individuals or small networks and require wider social organizing. At that point, the question is not only of social organization, but also of explicitly political organization; that is, organizing ourselves and our communities for political struggle. Sooner or later questions will emerge: Who will be saved? Who will pay the bill at the end of the day? Will finance companies, industry, and banks be saved as happened after the 2008 financial crisis at the expense of lives, homes, and the savings of common people? Or the other way around? The answers to these questions depend only on our capabilities to organize ourselves to defend our lives in all sectors of society.

The political perspective of pandemic communalism is to organize the emerging practical solidarity into a political force that can defend the interests and wellbeing of society against both the pandemic crisis and political threats emanating from it. Bank and corporate owners are already in attack mode, ready to blackmail for more money for themselves, while demanding "flexibility" and "sacrifice" from workers to secure their wealth. Sooner or later, their demands will intensify to include lower salaries, longer working hours, degenerate working conditions, and an obligation to work despite risking one's health and life.

When the epidemic starts to wither away, defending workers, the unemployed, and tenants against these attacks requires solidarity to take a form of coordinated action, such as strikes, protests, and blockades. Mutual aid can be developed in self-organized "counter logistics" that serve social needs regardless of the pressure from companies and their interest organizations.[8] The groups and neighbors that came together

via instant messaging and other apps can be the first step to organizing local structures of self-governance that are able to administer the life of the area's inhabitants and coordinate communally organized services.

Conclusions

It is important to point out that a pandemic communalism perspective is not only about the mitigation of crisis' symptoms. Instead, it is seeking a holistic solution based on the empowerment and defense of society by organizing and federating social initiatives, continuously expanding the sphere of democratic self-governance. To this end, the predominantly social nature of the pandemic must be analyzed correctly.

What is today called the coronavirus crisis is a multifaceted phenomenon and much deeper than the pandemic itself, which basically encompasses the whole of social life. The virus is from a biological source, but the development of COVID-19 from a local infection to a global crisis has mostly been due to social interactions and dynamics. The main dimensions of the corona crisis have been health care and social reproduction in general, economy, governance, and the relationship between nature and human society. Above all, these four fields determine the ongoing pandemic dynamics but also witness a deep and severe crisis. More precisely, the coronavirus revealed built-in malfunctions and flaws in the capitalist organization of these sectors of society and brought them to a premature dead end.

Unlike regional disasters such as earthquakes or hurricanes, a pandemic is not local, but affects whole societies. In the case of a pandemic, there is no wider functioning society that can give relief to a single community or locality hit by a disaster. A pandemic is too big and severe of a crisis for local and regional efforts or isolated relief initiatives of the people to handle. Meanwhile, it has also become clear that the ongoing crisis and the economic and ecological disasters looming just ahead of us cannot be solved by a superficial crisis management in the existing framework of states and markets. A sustainable solution must see the crisis as a whole and set in motion a profound transformation of society, and in the four central dimensions mentioned above. Lack of transformative development will inevitably lead to partial and inconclusive attempts that will not grasp the severity of the situation.

The question is no longer one of aiding the system, but rather constructing an alternative system while supporting people and communities.

Furthermore, any partiality or inconclusiveness in these critical times will only lead to continuation and repetition of economic, ecological, and health related crises while states of exception, lockdowns, technological surveillance tools, and other ad hoc measures will become a new normality.

Pandemic communalism is a proposition for such a conclusive solution. It is a perspective that is not limited either to the confines of states and markets or to the relative weakness of isolated relief and charity efforts. Pandemic communalism can be thought of as a third way, not surrendering to either side of this false dualism. It obviously emerges from local initiatives and builds itself around them, but if developed correctly, it will expand and take over more complicated social responsibilities and increase the sphere of popular self-administration in a democratic and federative way. Meanwhile, its relationship to the state system is a more antagonistic than a symbiotic one, although the two can also find temporary mutually beneficial relationships.

The communal character of pandemic communalism begins to be realized when different initiatives of mutual aid and community organizing link up with each other and relate to other initiatives of popular self-organization in a coordinated way. Federating different initiatives in a mutually beneficial, strengthening, and meaningful way is the real art of pandemic communalism and source of its power. Such an approach can be understood in the words of Murray Bookchin in his description of the "Meaning of Confederalism:"

> Confederalism, in effect, must be conceived as a whole: a consciously formed body of interdependencies that unites participatory democracy in municipalities with a scrupulously supervised system of coordination. It involves the dialectical development of independence and dependence into a more richly articulated form of interdependence [...] A choice between either self-sufficiency on the one hand or a market system of exchange on the other is a simplistic and unnecessary dichotomy.[9]

Pandemic Communalism can be thought of as the application of confederalist principles to our current situation of popular crisis organization. The centers or hubs of federalist coordination offer it a distinctive identity that can integrate a growing amount of people, community initiatives, civil society organizations, and other popular actors under a common roof. The resulting constellation is more than the sum of its parts and, therefore, the social power of federated initiatives does not increase linearly, but exponentially. The emerging communal and federal structure – and it alone – can lead Pandemic Communalism to become a real alternative that can reach a level of social organization required to overcome the ongoing crises.

Pandemic Communalism, as a federative and ever-expanding system of interdependencies, offers a framework in which different initiatives can connect with each other and coordinate their activities through popular self-management. When different initiatives federate themselves directly, without the mediation of state and market forces, the corrupting influence of capitalism weakens. It cannot approach each initiative individually and integrate them to the restoration of the old order. Instead, capitalism has to deal with a federated entity that has already started to establish principles, practices, mentalities, and even culture of their own. Thus, the question is no longer one of aiding the system, but rather constructing an alternative system while supporting people and communities. The development of an alternative is the true measure of Pandemic Communalism's development.

At the end of the day, going back to "normal," and how capitalism has transformed every aspect of our life, would be an unfortunate outcome of the corona crisis. Instead of figuring out how to return to a normal capitalist order, now is the perfect moment to start constructing an order of our own – one of wellbeing, freedom, and social ecology. People and nature can both be the winners of this crisis so long as we are able to reclaim our ability to self-govern our communal matters and relate to our environment in an ecological way. Ⓐ

Jean Desta is a pseudonym for a collective of European comrades working and focusing on different areas and social struggles. They are writers, academics, and researchers who are influenced by Murray Bookchin, Abdullah Öcalan and other authors in the quest for a revolutionary, libertarian socialist, and internationalist perspective for the twenty-first century.

Notes

1 Out of the Woods, "The Uses of Disaster," *Commune Magazine,* October 22, 2018, https://communemag.com/the-uses-of-disaster/

2 "Rent Strike? A Strategic Appraisal of Rent Strikes throughout History – and Today," transl. Crimethinc., March 30, 2020, https://crimethinc.com/2020/03/30/rent-strike-a-strategic-appraisal-of-rent-strikes-throughout-history-and-today

3 Alicia Adamczyk, "32% of U.S. households Missed Their July Housing Payments," CNBC, May 5, 2020, https://www.cnbc.com/2020/07/08/32-percent-of-us-households-missed-their-july-housing-payments.html

4 Commune, "It's Time to Build the Brigades," *Commune Magazine*, March 27, 2020, https://communemag.com/its-time-to-build-the-brigades/

5 Solidarity Brigades website: https://www.brigades.info/

6 Economist, "The market v. the real economy," *The Economist*, May 7, 2020, https://www.economist.com/leaders/2020/05/07/the-market-v-the-real-economy

7 "Coronavirus: Amazon Workers Strike over Virus Protection," BBC, March 31, 2020, https://www.bbc.com/news/business-52096273

8 Anonymous, *Short Circuit – A Counterlogistics Reader* (No New Perspectives, 2015).

9 Murray Bookchin, "The Meaning of Confederalism," *Green Perspectives* 20 (1990).

TAKING TIME, BUILDING POWER: OUR QUARANTINE BOOK CLUB

WHEN THE FIRST WAVE OF COVID-19 HIT THE PACIFIC NORTHWEST in March of 2020, a few things quickly became clear to us: we'd be spending a lot more time at home, we'd be hungry for the human connection that usually sustains us, and our friends in the arts were getting hammered in terms of their income and job prospects. As a way of addressing all three at once while building non-hierarchal power together, we started the Quarantine Book Club. Below is a transcript of all the communication from our first round. It ends with our first dispatch for our second round, to give you a sense of where and how it extends.

We began Our Quarantine Book Club by reading Junauda Petrus's *The Stars and the Blackness Between Them*. Junauda is a Minneapolis-based Black queer author, performer, and artist who we met through one of her artistic collaborators, another amazing Minneapolis-based author and organizer named Erin Sharkey. When the pandemic started, Junauda was beginning promotion for the book. Knowing so many people we knew but couldn't see right now wanted to read her book made it an obvious first choice, and we quickly assembled a network of folks via our personal social media accounts.

The book club pretty much just consists of an email account and the time we spent together. As you'll see below, we spent a few weeks responding to some prompts as we worked through the book. Then, the first round culminated with a video chat meeting where book club members got to meet with Junauda and talk to her about the book. We pooled money via an app to make sure she got compensated, but everybody had so much fun on the call that it felt much more valuable than money.

Our group was spread from Oakland and Bellingham to Minneapolis, Buffalo, and Boston and all the way to Poland. We brought each other life through this act of connection across the often-deadening medium of the internet. We came together consensually, without hierarchies, officers, a charter, or any funding, just to bask in the glow we can create when we come together with enthusiasm and intention. We recharged each other while combining our energies to lift up an important contemporary cultural producer who gave us the power through her literature to understand the links between everything from astrology to abolition.

Pick up a copy of *The Stars and the Blackness Between Them*, peruse the dispatches we wrote together below, and email QuarantineBookClub@gmail.com if you want to stay updated or join.

—Josh Cerretti for the Quarantine Book Club

Quarantine Book Club
Dispatch #1

Hey everybody,

Welcome to Quarantine Book Club, where you don't actually have to be under quarantine to participate but we're not gonna meet in person anyway!

Here's how it works: Over the next two weeks, we'll be sending out prompts with increasing frequency that solicit your thoughts as we collectively read Junauda Petrus' *The Stars and the Blackness Between Them*. We'll share your responses in these emails and you can participate as much or as little as you like.

On or around April 1st, we'll have a whole group video chat with Junauda where you can ask her any questions you have about the book or her work. We're eventually going to ask you for a $5–$15 sliding scale donation that will go directly to Junauda for her participation, which we seek to compensate fairly during this tough time for many artists. If you have particular time constraints that day, let us know and we'll try to schedule around that as best as we can.

So, let us know if you have any questions, but without further ado, you'll find the first prompt below. Looking forward to this!

– J + T

Quarantine Book Club Prompt #1: The first thing everybody needs to do is a get access to the book: buy a physical copy or ebook, get it from a library, or let us know if you can't afford access and we'll get something figured out. Once you have a copy, in whatever format you've got it in, snap a selfie with the cover or a picture of the book in the environment in which you'll read it – you can post it to social media with the hashtag #quarantinebookclub or just email it to us so we can compose our first group photo.

Some say it's a major no-no to judge a book by it's cover, but that's exactly what we'll ask you to do next. Along with your photo, share your first impressions of *The Stars and the Blackness Between Them* based on the title, cover art, and anything else you're feeling going in before you turn the first page. Whether it's one sentence or a whole page of thoughts, we want to hear what you're thinking going in.

To give everybody time to track down a copy and because we're still adding participants, we'll give everyone until MIDNIGHT (west coast) THURSDAY MARCH 19TH to send their picture and cover thoughts.

The next Dispatch will be on Friday but, in the meantime, happy reading!

Quarantine Book Club
Dispatch #2

Hey friendly friends,
We're here with your second dispatch from Quarantine Book Club, bringing you the first round of responses from you all and a new prompt to try out with the first part of the book.

If you read the last email carefully, you know this one is a little later than expected, and that's because the philosophy of Quarantine Book Club is life happens, take it at your own pace, no cop shit. This isn't a class or an obligation, so participate as much as it feeds you at the times that you've got the time and nobody is going to hassle you about it either way. That means send your response to Prompt #1 any time and we'll still include it, also feel free to respond to anything anyone says in their responses.

With that, here's the responses we got to the first prompt and, at the bottom, Prompt #2.

– T + J

First off, what an excellent group of people: (follow our instagram, @ourquarantinebookclub if you're into that sort of thing)

From A:

This cover art makes me think of magic and a sweet connection that exists between the two protagonists. It invites the reader to witness an intimate moment shared by these women that appears frozen in time as if it was infinite. Their bodies are comfortably stretched across the water surface and surrounded by water lilies, stars and the moonshine. This moment is filled with a certain promise of happiness, joy, love for each other, longing and desire.

From C:

I love the vibes of the cover illustration. The colors are gorgeous. The characters' body image and facial expression communicate such a peaceful ease with themselves and each other.

From D:

I am so excited to read this book! I basically trust J's reading recommendations a bunch, (and I have every reason to trust T's recommendations tho I don't yet know her very well!) and I really like the idea of a quarantine book club. One of my original hopes for this strange season was to catch up on reading a stack of mostly nonfiction I've been accumulating for my job over the last few years, but realistically I'll have a better time doing that if I'm also doing some reading in community with folks. (And who knows what my professional and personal time will even look like in this season!) It's been an unusually long time since I've settled into a good novel, and so I'm mostly excited for that as well!

In terms of the cover itself: my first assumption is that this is a graphic novel, which is great, and I was only a little disappointed when it turned out not to be. But I wonder if that's a deliberate choice for the cover, to evoke some of the drama and, I don't know, emotional tone of comics as a medium. I love the title, and especially after I read the summary on the publisher's website, I loved the energy of the cover. I feel very excited to get to know these characters and see how they will connect! Rachael asked about what kind of book I was starting and I said I think it's like, queer teen African Diaspora romance. We'll see if I'm at all accurate but I'm excited to find out! <3

From J:

The cover is giving me some real Earthseed / *Parable of the Sower* vibes. It also looks like it could be the cover to a graphic novel. The title and the images of the characters on the cover make me feel like it's going to be a love story. I don't read a lot of YA so I'm looking forward to a different style than I'm usually reading.

From J:
Thoughts on the cover: A queer sci-fi romance novel.

From J:
I'm most into the subtle sprinkle of stars across what seems like both the plane of the galaxy and the bed that the characters are laying on. The font and background definitely give it that epic *Star Wars* kind of vibe, but it's chill and relational instead of high-octane and militarized. I haven't thought deeply about the connections between the blackness of the universe's vastness and racial Blackness so I'm interested to see how it's explored here.

Junauda Petrus

From S:
My first impressions of the book:
    – the title got me thinking about the fact that the blackness is the whole; the stars are pinpricks in its fabric, but it is the whole. The story of Blackness, too, is the whole, even though we pretend like it's the stars. It's the foundation, it's the backdrop, it's the very inception of human life and all of human history.
    – the cover art takes me back to that time of fond remembrance, of discovery, that longing that is at once so painful and so pleasurable when it comes to first love, even first real friendship. It is a time of possibility, unsullied by heartbreak, yet also a time of maturity, when you've still lived long enough to be bullied, to be told that who you are is not right, to be reminded that your place in the world is overshadowed & controlled by people and forces more powerful (though no smarter) than you.
    – generally, I CANNOT wait to get into this book and discuss it with you! I've had the pleasure of hearing Junauda read excerpts at an event, and I have been waiting and waiting for more!

From Z:
I know nothing at all about this book, so my first impressions are truly uninformed:
    I'm curious about whether or not, and hopeful, that this book will involve a discussion of modern Blackness. Especially as it pertains to young Black women.
    Is this book going to be science fiction? Dystopian? Set in the modern day? The cover could indicate any and all of the above. Maybe it's all

three! Nothing like a good time travel book to get through quarantine...

Is it a queer Black love story??? I can't wait.

Quarantine Book Club Prompt #2: Now that you're getting started, we'd like you to share a response to any or all of these questions relating to the first eighty-three pages of *The Stars and the Blackness Between Them* (Cancer and Leo Seasons).

First off, astrology clearly plays a big role here, so just drop your sign and whatever we need to know about that.

Second, we're brought to two distant but linked settings in the early chapters of the book: Trinidad and and the Twin Cities. So what's your connection or conception of these places? How did Junauda bring them to life or make you see them differently than you thought before?

Third, we're following an account of being a teenager, which sort of places this book in the potentially controversial category of young adult literature. What about the book so far feels like it fits in the YA category and what about the book exceeds what you've come to expect from the genre? What's appealing, too true, or not quite right about how Junauda depicts being seventeen? What do you think about the relationships between adults and children in the novel? How does this story about adolescence make you feel about when you were a teenager or being a teenager today?

Fourth and finally, music plays a big role throughout *The Stars and the Blackness Between Them*. If you haven't noticed the playlist suggested at the very end of the book, we suggest listening sometime as you read. What's your favorite musical reference in the book so far?

Again, share your thoughts whether they relate to the prompt or not sometime on or before THURSDAY APRIL 2ND and we'll get the next dispatch out soon after that.

Quarantine Book Club
Dispatch #3

Hey everybody,

I hope you're safely and comfortably self-isolating while you dive into *The Stars and the Blackness Between Them*. Below you'll find some responses to the last prompt and new one for this week. Most importantly, here's some info about our live conversation with the author herself:

Quarantine Book Club will host a Zoom with Junauda Petrus on Sunday, April 12th from 4–5:30pm (CENTRAL time) to discuss her book *The Stars and the Blackness Between Them*. Everybody will get a chance to introduce themselves and ask a question of Junauda, we hope to also have plenty of time for discussion between us all. We are asking for a $5–$15 sliding scale donation, with 100% of the money going directly to Junauda to help her get some extra income when so many artists are struggling with cancellations and closings.

To participate you'll need an OK internet connection and you'll probably want to download the Zoom app in advance. To receive the link for the chat, you can Venmo T or email the bookclub address to set up an alternate method if Venmo isn't your thing. If you're out of work or otherwise can't afford to donate but want to participate, you can also email back to request the link and we aren't going to ask any questions or shut you out of the discussion.

Prompt #3 for Quarantine Book Club is this: Having finished the book (or even if you haven't yet), what question do you want to ask the author? What was most memorable, exciting, or confusing about the book to you? What are you wondering that didn't get answered within the pages we got? What are you wondering about the process of making *The Stars and the Blackness Between Them* or Junauda's other work? You don't have to peer-review with the group first, but it never hurts! Email anytime before midnight on Saturday and we'll share responses with the reminder email Sunday morning. We'll also share responses to old prompts.

Let us know if you have any questions and enjoy the responses to the second prompt below!

– J + T

From S:
1. I'm a Pisces, through and through. Always fighting the opposite sides of me, in everything.

2. Trinidad has been on my bucket list for a LONG time and I live & love in the TC. My conception of Trinidad has been amplified and enhanced; I loved visualizing the scenery and "meeting" the characters who make the place a whole. Later, being introduced to the Ital recipes, I was able to add an imagined taste to the sights and smells I'd encountered through Audre. Damn, I want to be there NOW, like her!

Black Eden sounds and seems idyllic; a place I don't recognize right now, but probably will in August, sans Mabel's dad's gorgeous garden!

3. Of course, the main characters being teens, the strong presence of parent figures and the thoughts they're experiencing fit well with YA. Yet I appreciate the nuance Junauda threads into the smallest things: the philosophical thoughts, their observations of the people they're attracted to, and even how they view their parents makes these protagonists' seem mature beyond their years. I especially felt this in the opening chapters where we meet Audre and Queenie. Being in the characters' heads allows me to see their perspectives and distill it through my own

adult experiences and lenses, offering perhaps a different view than a younger reader might have.

4. I'm very curious to check out the band we meet at the start of the book; I didn't realize there was a playlist! What a lovely thought!

From J:

I'm an Aquarius and have always been generally satisfied with the description of us as flowy weirdos, so I've never felt like I needed to dig much deeper into repping my rising/moon signs.

I've never been to Trinidad, closest I've been is the Caribbean part of Costa Rica, but I've spent a bunch of time in the Twin Cities and I love how the book brings them and the people of the city to life. I feel like my whole life I've been bombarded with stories set in NYC, Southern California, sometimes maybe Chicago or San Francisco. Basically all the cultural production about cities in the second tier of population is obscure and regional, so I really appreciate getting out of that mode.

I don't read much YA, honestly pretty much just *The Hunger Games* so I didn't feel out of the zeitgeist, which means I don't have the firmest frame in which to put this, but I like how the teen characters know what the fuck is going on. They're appropriately angsty and naive for teenagers but they aren't dummies and they understand so much of their own world that the adults around them can't process. They even seem to know the adults better than they know themselves.

I feel like the purple liner for this book is pure Prince tribute, so I've been humming "Baby I'm a Star" a lot while reading.

From J:

Astrology: I'm a virgo sun, taurus rising, virgo moon. Big earth sign energy.

I love reading more about Trinidad! My good friend Michél grew up there and has described a lot of different things to me, especially the food. My next door neighbors are Rastas (from Jamaica though) and I've had the chance to eat Ital a few times so I got excited to see that reference. They even have a vanity license plate that says ITAL. Junauda brings so much to life through describing food! I've spent a little time in the Twin Cities, mostly it makes me think of my friend Ed who just died – we were in St. Paul for his funeral in early March. I'm realizing I have a pretty narrow (white) perspective on the area so the book has this whole Black world that's new to me.

What makes it feel like YA to me is the centering of teenage characters. Audre and Mabel have depth and are given the chance to tell their own stories. There's a lot that rings true to me from an emotional perspective – Audre's pain in particular cuts so deep in a way that sounds familiar from when I was a teenager and just isn't as accessible now as a thirty-nine-year-old. I haven't read a ton of YA but what I have has been romance, dystopian, or a combo of the two – and Junauda transcends what I usually think of as romance and makes it as beautiful and painful as it can really feel. Without anybody killing anyone (at least not yet).

There's a longer playlist on spotify that Junauda put up that I've been listening to and it's giving me renewed love/joy about Whitney Houston.

Quarantine Book Club
Dispatch #4

Hey folks,

One last reminder on today's chat with a couple more responses about the book below.

See you this afternoon!

– J + T

From A:

First of all, Junauda – thank you so much for this beautiful gift.

Reading *The Stars and the Blackness Between Them* has resonated with me in more ways that I could have imagined. I have lived in the U.S. for ten years and had to go back to Poland a little over a year ago because well immigration and Trump... leaving behind the woman I love and trying to figure things out for the time being. What I love about this book is that instead of focusing on non-belonging, it captures all those moments of connection among people and a potential that lies buried in every single person waiting to resurface – like Mabel's dying wish: a selfless gesture and an attempt to free somebody else, Audre's connection to Queenie and her ancestors through her desire to heal Mabel, Neri's embracing her queerness, freeing herself from her family and having a fresh start with random (or not so random) people she meets. To me the book is about freedom and acceptance of who you are, where you came from and what you came here to do. If the category YA fiction will help the book reach a wider audience among young people, I am all for it. Everyone should read it.

Also, the book seamlessly weaves in so many important questions: the fear of growing up queer in heteronormative worlds, a terminal disease, the fear of death, the carceral state and Blackness, Audre's "migratory subjectivity," the ancestors, the spirit world, the earth, the sky and the sea. What stands out to me in this book is how Junauda has created this web of connections among all of the protagonists, life and the vision of afterlife through Queenie and through astrology – reading into the universe which connects us all. Thank you for the butterflies. I could not have imagined a better conclusion to this beautiful story.

As for the question I would like to raise during our conversation: In the book, America seems very accepting of queerness as opposed to Trinidad and I am curious to learn more about how you see this distinction.
Previous questions:

- Astrologically, I am a Cancer – caring, nurturing, loving and moodier than I would like to be lol but made peace with that a long time ago.

- Trinidad & Twin Cities: I have never been to either one of those places but really wanted to go to Trinidad. The closest I've been are the Dominican Republic, Puerto Rico, Jamaica and Panama. Having read the book when I think of Trinidad now I see Queenie's house on top of the hill overlooking the ocean.

- What fits the YA genre are the insights into what teenagers do and how they perceive the world around them but to me it way surpasses this category. I am not that familiar with the genre but at a guess the problems these teenagers are facing are not about school life, people at school they have to put up with etc. but existential questions they are raising.

- Musical reference – I grew up listening to Whitney Houston in Poland in the 90s. She was one of the few American artist (and Tina Turner!) who came here right after communism had ended and she will always have a special place in my heart. And, I am all the way a Janelle Monáe girl.

From C:
Signs: Pisces sun, Scorpio Moon, Taurus Rising. More watery and emotional on the inside, others see me as more grounded and strong than I feel.

From Y:
Many aspects of Audre and Mabel's adolescent experience rang very true to me, like the intensity of their developing values, politics, romances and sexuality as well as their passion for music.

I read most of the book pre-pandemic and am just getting around to finishing it before the conversation tomorrow and also vow to look up the playlist and immerse myself in the music too. I may end up re-reading the whole thing, since my memory isn't great in general and current events are taking up a lot of my mental bandwidth and I know I will appreciate even more about it reading it in a less disjointed way.

My questions for Junauda would be: Tell us about your decisions to include additional narrators from older generations (Afua's chapters and Queenie-dream scenes?) later on in the book.

The first round of our book club culminated in mid-April, as the pandemic hit its first peak in many of the places we reside, with a group video

CHRIS LIGHT, *TREE FIGHTING CAPITALISM*

*chat about the book starring the author. Over the course of ninety minutes,
about twenty people built a network of powerful ideas about abolition,
Blackness, queerness, youth, and so much more. We delighted in seeing
some familiar faces as well as in meeting some new comrades for the first
time. All the participants transferred a few dollars based on what they
could afford and we got to compensate Junauda for writing this amazing
book, going along with our idea without hesitation, and connecting with
everyone on the call with such ease and wisdom that we all walked away
feeling more powerful. The Quarantine Book Club is a small spark, one
dim flicker in the increasingly bleak nightmarescape of heteropatriarchal*

racial crapitalism, but the old adage "better to light a candle than curse the darkness" holds true. The current pandemic and the more enduring systems of exploitation we live within leave so many of us feeling helpless and disempowered, but at the same time many of us are starting from where we're at and building power however we can. Who knows what sparks might light the flames that power us toward a better future? Until then, here's what's next...

Quarantine Book Club
Dispatch #5

Greetings All,

Welcome to the second installment of Quarantine Book Club, a low-pressure and low-stakes group where we read a book together, discuss a bit over email, and then chat together once sometime in the future!

Last time around, we got the chance to share Junauda Petrus's beautiful *The Stars and the Blackness Between Them*. We had a fun, nourishing, and smile-inducing conversation together with Junauda at the end.

This Round's Pick and Additional Info

For our second installation, Theresa has volunteered to facilitate and she's chosen Kristen Millares Young's debut novel *Subduction* as our pick for this second time around. I know shipping status for lots of things is slowed down right now – if you're looking for a copy of the book, you can order directly from Red Hen Press, including a $9.99 eBook version if you're into that.

While you're waiting for your book to arrive, I've included some other materials for your perusal to give you a feel for its contents:

First, check out the amazing visual book trailer that gives you the feel for the PNW coast, which features prominently in the story. Then, you can read this beautiful interview with Kristen, where she talks about memory, voyeurism, responsibility, and space. If your palette has been whetted by that, check out her website too, where she links all kinds of exciting reviews and reflections on the novel. Lastly, I attached a brief essay for you all by Tlingit writer Ernestine Hayes called "Contemporary Creative Writing and Ancient Oral Tradition" that talks about the importance of understanding place as a character rather than a lifeless setting.

All of these will prime you well if/while you're waiting for your book to arrive and will definitely add some depth and texture to your reading if you're already all up in it!

Prompt #1 for *SUBDUCTION*

Second verse, same as the first – let's start with first impressions.

If you have the book, what is your response to the cover? What does it invoke for you and what does it make you think the book will be about?

If you don't have the book yet, check out the trailer above. Same question.

You can reply to this email with your responses. I'll aim to send the second dispatch in the next two weeks, so send back your thoughts around then. I'll send a reminder email too.

Reminders

This is a low-stakes, low-pressure experience. There are no hard deadlines and we each work to our own capacity when and if we can. Emails might be late, responses might be overlapped or limited or nonexistent. No worries, no one is coming after you or disappointed or upset. No cop shit.

Super excited to read with y'all again and reach out if you have any questions, want to add someone to the email list, or want to volunteer to facilitate the next one!

Talk soon,
TW + QBC

MUTUAL AID TOP 5s
WHAT KEPT US GOING THIS YEAR?

What are your top five things that have brought you comfort and/or joy during the past year? It can be anything, foods, movies, people, animals, thoughts, books, records, yoga positions, a particular hike, a new pen, an old friend, whatever!

Sam Smith
Perspectives copy editor & second reader

- The uncanny abundance of my tiny backyard garden in Brooklyn
- Unexpected letters from friends in far-away places
- Friendships struck up in the streets
- The often-murky Atlantic Ocean at Rockaway Beach, to which I've grown closer than ever
- Baking lavish desserts (even when my cat is the only one around to appreciate them!).

Hilary Lazar
Perspectives collective member

- Getting so much more time with my kiddo and partner that I wouldn't have had otherwise (fuck the daily grind under capitalism)
- Feeling inspired and strengthened by all the amazing mutual aid projects and BLM uprising (another world *is* possible!)
- Slowing down, noticing the birds in our yard, taking neighborhood walks, and exploring local trails and lakes (reconnecting with nature and masked up adventures with friends can be pretty great)
- Finding my inner crafter, baker, and gardener (I'm a pandemic cliché)
- Working on *Perspectives* and the "Pandemics from the Bottom Up" online issue!

Maia Ramnath
Perspectives collective member
- Reconnecting with bike riding
- Voices of hawks and crows outside my house in the morning
- Ben & Jerry's
- Multiple *Star Wars* TV series
- Witnessing the collective will, imagination, and courage to change; the hope that since everything status quo has broken down anyway, how we grow back can be different

Charles Weigl
AK Press
- A new kitten
- More naps
- Restarting a writing practice
- Silence
- Never worrying about being somewhere

Theresa Warburton
Perspectives collective member
- Getting sick of and finally ignoring my phone
- Writing texts like letters
- The five-minute check-in with faraway friends, especially during uprisings
- Books about witches
- Movie franchises that prevent me from having to make decisions about what to watch next

Charles Overbeck
Eberhardt Press
- Comrades
- Monster energy drinks (to survive night demos)
- YouTube videos (string theory, neurological disorders, Rachel Maddow, WWII tank battles, etc.)
- Gorilla Glue #4
- Gardening

YOU SAY YOU WANT A REVOLUTION?

JAMES MUMM

THERE IS A CENTURIES-LONG CONVERSATION ON HOW BEST TO achieve transformational change, taken up here in a dialogue between authors with insight and ideas for today's political revolutionaries. Almost 150 years ago, the Farmers Alliance organized two million people in the United States by rallying an army of unpaid lecturers – forty thousand of them – and starting a thousand newspapers. Let's sit with this for a moment. With communications methods that we would now call "antiquated" or limited, the Farmers Alliance organized more than 3 percent of the US population. Clearly, there is still much we can learn from looking at that movement and classic works like Lawrence Goodwyn's *The Populist Moment: A Short History of the Agrarian Revolt in America* (1978).

In fact, the Farmers Alliance, and the Populist movement more broadly, came incredibly close to attaining the critical 3.5 percent population threshold that Erica Chenoweth and Maria Stephan found to presage revolutionary change in their landmark study of nonviolent resistance. Chenoweth and Stephan's study focuses on "three specific, intense, and extreme forms of resistance:[1] anti-regime, anti-occupation, and secession campaigns," but there are lessons for people interested in transformational change in modern democracies and republics.

Through analysis of 323 violent and nonviolent resistance campaigns between 1900 and 2006, in *Why Civil Resistance Works: The Strategic Logic of Nonviolent Conflict* (2016), Chenoweth and Stephan seek to explain "two related phenomena: why nonviolent resistance often succeeds relative to violent resistance, and under what conditions, non-violent resistance succeeds or fails."[2] Furthermore, what they consider most striking "is that between 1900 and 2006, nonviolent resistance campaigns were nearly twice as likely to achieve full or partial success as their violent counterparts."[3] Their research has been foundational to mobilizations like Extinction Rebellion.

Tear gas fills the park across from the Justice Center during the 2020 uprising in Portland.

Building on these findings, Mark and Paul Engler's *This Is an Uprising: How Nonviolent Revolt is Shaping the Twenty-First Century* (2016) explores momentum-driven movements that stretch from the Salt March to the Birmingham Children's Crusade and from Otpor to Occupy. Momentum is the name for an approach to social change that seeks to give progressive organizers the tools and frameworks to build massive, decentralized movements. Like Chenoweth and Stephan, they find that strategic nonviolence serves as a powerful tool for social change. And we round out this chorus of voices with adrienne maree brown's *Emergent Strategy: Shaping Change, Changing Worlds* (2017), which brings a personal reflection on a life in activism into the conversation. Although coming from a very different perspective and approach, in *Emergent Strategy*, she addresses several of the most challenging questions at the heart of transformational change: "What we are all really asking … is how do we, who know the world needs to change, begin to practice being different? How do we have to be for justice to truly be transformative?"

Read together, these four texts bring us into this long-standing conversation on transformational movement building and help us to understand what works, what doesn't, and, above all, what we should be doing today if we want to see real change.

What Doesn't Work?

So, what do these authors say definitely does not work? Let's start with Goodwyn:

> Unfortunately, history does not support the notion that mass protest movements develop because of hard times. Depressed economies or exploitive arrangements of power and privilege may produce lean years or even lean lifetimes for millions of people, but the historical evidence is conclusive that they do not produce mass political insurgency. The simple fact of the matter is that, in ways that affect mind and body, times have been "hard" for most humans throughout human history and for most of that period people have not been in rebellion.[4]

That's our lesson number one: *civil resistance doesn't happen just because times are hard.*

Chenoweth and Stephan, meanwhile, assert that

> nonviolent campaigns fail to achieve their objectives when they are unable to overcome the challenge of participation, when they fail to recruit a robust, diverse, and broad-based membership that can erode the power base

of the adversary and maintain resilience in the face of repression.[5]

That's lesson number two: while you need mass participation, *the quality of mass participation – robust, diverse, broad-based – can be more important than the quantity.*

Adrienne marie brown further suggests that "[u]prisings and resistance and mass movement require a tolerance of messiness, a tolerance of many, many paths being walked on at once."[6]

This, then, is our lesson number three: *don't shy away from messiness and complexity in organization and movement building.*

What Does Work

Now, let's dig into what these authors say *does* work to create lasting transformational change, so we are all better prepared. In *This Is a Nonviolent Uprising*, Engler and Engler comment:

> What if periods of mass, spontaneous uprising are neither as spontaneous nor as unbridled as they might at first appear? What if the fits of social change that burst into our headlines like flash storms can actually be forecast? What if one can read the clouds and understand their signs? Or what if, in fact, it is possible to influence the weather? … Can versions of civil resistance be used to confront the challenges of climate change, runaway economic inequality, racial injustice, and the corporate hijacking of government?

Now *that* is an intriguing question.

Returning to Goodwyn, the Populist revolt had four stages of democratic movement building. These stages, in fact, resonate across the historical examples shared by Chenoweth and Stephan – Burma, Iran, the Philippines, and the Palestinian Territories – as well as the stories from India, Serbia, and the US shared by the Englers.

Goodwyn breaks down these stages for us:

(1) the creation of an autonomous institution where new interpretations can materialize that run counter to those of prevailing authority – a development which, for the sake of simplicity, we may describe as "movement forming;"

(2) the creation of a tactical means to attract masses of people – i.e. "movement recruiting;"

(3) the achievement of a heretofore culturally unsanctioned level of social analysis – "movement educating;" and

(4) the creation of an institutional means whereby the new ideas, shared now by the rank and file of the mass movement, can be expressed in an autonomous political way – "movement politicized."[8]

These four movement stages also have some preconditions: individual self-respect, collective self-confidence, and an agenda. Together these form the foundational building blocks for transformational change: a "movement culture." Goodwyn describes this as "a spirit of egalitarian hope, expressed in the actions of two million beings – not in the prose of a platform, however creative, and not, ultimately, even in the third party, but in a self-generated culture of collective dignity and individual longing."[9]

So as to come up with a unified theory of transformational change, let us first explore the elements of movement culture that these authors uncover in their historical analyses and personal experiences, then we will draw them together and end with a challenge to would-be changemakers.

The Englers draw our focus to how "Gandhi struggled throughout his life with creating a hybrid" that generated a movement culture built from this mix of economic cooperatives, bold platforms, and political education. They elaborate:

> He (Gandhi) was famous for his campaigns of widespread civil disobedience, or *satyagraha*. But he combined these with an ongoing "constructive program," through which local communities could build autonomy, as well as with efforts to build the grassroots reach of the Indian National Congress, which became the country's leading independence organization.[10]

A strikingly similar mix was created by the Populists in their summer encampments, wagon trains, and sub-alliance (smaller than a county) meetings, which Goodwyn describes as "unsteepled places of worship."[11] And "movement culture" was at the center of the civil rights movement of the 1950s and 1960s too, when nightly mass meetings in Black churches served as its beating heart.

Movement culture is created when people need each other to win their own freedom, and they are willing to engage in collective sacrifice and actions that reinforce their solidarity. Brown has another word for this: "emergent strategy: strategy for building complex patterns and systems of change through relatively small interactions, is to me – the potential scale of transformation that could come from movements intentionally practicing this adaptive, relational way of being, on our own and with others."[12]

Notably, as evident in these authors' discussions, movement culture can also generate strategic and tactical innovation when campaigns have

Federal troops assaulting demonstrators at the US Courthouse in Portland.

broad-scale diversity and breadth of participants. "Because tactical innovation occurs on the fringes of a movement," Chenoweth and Stephan contend, "campaigns with larger numbers of participants, and consequently wider margins, are more likely to produce tactical innovations."[13] They are careful to say that participation can take the form of both concentrated and dispersed (stay-aways, sit-ins, occupations, economic boycotts) civil resistance. They continue:

> Higher levels of participation contribute to a number of mechanisms necessary for success, including enhanced resilience, higher probabilities of tactical innovation, expanded civic disruption (thereby raising the costs to the regime of maintaining the status quo), and loyalty shifts involving the opponent's erstwhile supporters, including members of the security forces.[14]

Furthermore, if participants are the body, then training and political education are the lifeblood of movement culture. As the Englers explain about the civil society movement in Serbia's return to democracy, "[t]he influx of new participants presented a challenge for Otpor."[15] They ask:

> ... How would it immerse large numbers of people in its organizational culture and have them understand the guidelines that allowed its decentralized teams to

be effective? The organization's answer was mass training... In a very short amount of time, people could go
from being total outsiders to becoming team leaders in
their towns. And the training process was exponential.
New chapters were outfitted with manuals and toolkits
enabling them to host their own trainings.[16]

The transmission of movement culture is, above all else, relational.
It is cultivated in the collective experience of nonviolent direct action,
economic cooperation against the grain of capitalism, political education, and training. These require intentional relationship building and
the forging of bonds based on collective self-interest.

Goodwyn describes how the Populists organized two million people
through a distributed organizing program of "lecturers" and "lecturing
schools" to propagate political education and cooperative economics.
He details how the Populist Alliance created a movement culture in
over forty thousand sub-alliances across rural America in the course of
building its structure of economic cooperation. As he explains it:

That idea – at the very heart of the movement culture
– was a profoundly simple one: the Populists believed
they could work together to be free individually. In their
institutions of self-help, Populists developed and acted
upon a crucial democratic insight: to be encouraged to
surmount rigid cultural inheritances and to act with
autonomy and self-confidence, individual people need
the psychological support of other people. The people
need to "see themselves" experimenting in new democratic forms.[17]

The Englers similarly identify this same strange and combustive
alchemy of movement culture in the momentum-driven mobilizations
they studied. "Time and again, in uprisings that steal the spotlight and

illuminate injustices that are otherwise ignored, we see three elements – disruption, sacrifice, and escalation – combining in forceful ways."[18]

A Unified Theory of Transformational Change

Movement culture is the force that holds together a unified theory of transformational change – the long-term agenda framework. It is what we need to realize broad-scale transformation.

To achieve transformational change, first we need to leverage this movement culture to change the landscape within which we operate. This is the work of both the civil resistance campaigns that Chenoweth and Stephan describe as well as the Englers' momentum-driven mobilizations. Since we are fighting on terrain defined by the corporate-conservative radical Right, we need to first transform our landscape through this movement culture and how it leads to movement moments, electoral change, and shifting the dominant narrative. This requires escalating power through organized people, money, and ideas.

Power is the meeting place between mass protest and people's organizations, between changing the landscape and making structural transformations of economies and societies. To win lasting, radical social change that shifts power from corporations and the wealthy to people and the public starts with what may feel like incremental change – but this is only if you are not truly paying close enough attention. In reality, these are stepping stones toward increasingly structural reforms.

A word of caution – we're not alone here in trying to do this. The radical Right is also trying to win its own form of transformational change and has its own movement culture. Incremental changes – often imperceptible stepping stones – have proven tremendously effective in advancing the right-wing agenda. This is how the radical Right came to prominence in the United States over the last several decades, and how they are now working to undermine democracies around the world.

CHRISTOPHER FRANCISCO (DINÉ)

According to Chenoweth and Stephan, it makes sense the radical Right would take aim at democracy, as open societies have built-in mechanisms for reform. And, in many parts of the world, the Right is winning and democracy is being beaten into retreat.

When we win structural victories, however, we institutionalize the change we seek. There is a dynamic relationship between changing the landscape, winning structural reforms and building power: a combination of all three are necessary to create lasting, structural transformations. The climax of struggle is not the end of the mobilization or civil resistance campaign – it is the structural transfer of power that can institutionalize new democratic and economic relationships.

Goodwyn gets this spot on when he writes:

> If the central task of democratic reform involves finding a way to oppose the received hierarchical culture with a newly created democratic culture, and if, as the Alliance experience reveals, progress toward this culminating climax necessarily must build upon prior stages of political and organizational evolution that have the effect of altering the political perspectives of millions of people, then democratic movements, to be successful, clearly require a high order of sequential achievement.[19]

It's not helpful to think of a sharp division of labor between the movements and organizations that struggle for transformational change, and those trying to institutionalize structural reforms. They may follow different "rules for radicals" to achieve varied goals, but as demonstrated by the historical examples shared by these authors, effective movement organizations can do – and have done – both. The Englers, for instance, lift up movement organizations such as the Southern Christian Leadership Conference and Otpor as "hybrid organizations" with the ability to code-switch as they respond to the needs of the political moment. Chenoweth and Stephan point to formations such as the *hay'at i madhabi*, neighborhood religious associations that were linked to mosques (12,000 in Tehran alone), as critical spaces where the social forces in the anti-regime campaign forged their national alliance in Iran.

The Path Forward

This brings us back to the big challenge in front of us here in the United States: addressing the root causes of racial capitalism and forging a winning alliance of forces that can innovate and win structural transformation.

Goodwyn zeroes in on the critical urgency of this:

> [T]he American tradition of white supremacy cast a forbidding shadow over the prospect of uniting black

and white tenants, sharecroppers, and smallholders into an enduring political force across the South. … In an era of transcendent white racism, the curbing of "vicious corporate monopoly" did not carry for black farmers the ring of salvation it had for white agrarians. It was the whiteness of corporate monopoly – and the whiteness of those who wanted to trim the power of the monopolists – that worried Negroes. Both sets of white antagonists lived by the values of the American caste system … Before the black man could worry about economic injustice, he had to worry about survival.[20]

In America, this extends to our movement building as well – people are molded by the contours of race, and how peoples' organizations institutionalize the leadership of women, people of color, trans people and others facing oppression. Goodwyn further captures both the success and failures of Populist multiracial movements:

> Black lecturers who ranged over the South organizing state and local Alliances did not enter Southern towns behind fluttering flags and brass bands. They attempted to organize slowly and patiently, seeking out the natural leaders in rural black communities and building from there. … Nevertheless, white supremacy hung over the organization with a brooding presence that ultimately proved suffocating. The reason was simple: white supremacy prevented black farmers from performing the kinds of collective public acts essential to the creation of an authentic movement culture.[21]

In *Emergent Strategy,* brown also points to the need for small incremental change and the critical need to address race in our struggles for change. She reflects on fractals in nature as a way to propose how we can move forward in 2021 for transformational change. She says, evoking the way these natural patterns unfold, that "what we practice at the small scale sets the patterns for the whole system."[22] In other words, if we, as organizers, are intentional about building multiracial, urban–rural and intersectional movements, then this should show up in all of the relationships and spaces where we are present. She continues with the aspirational call: "I would call our work to change the world 'science fictional behavior' – being concerned with the way our actions and beliefs now, today, will shape the future, tomorrow, the next generations."[23]

Goodwyn, although looking at the past, lands in a similar place. He describes how

> in their struggle to build their cooperative commonwealth, in their "joint notes of the brotherhood," in their

mass encampments, their rallies, their wagon trains, their meals for thousands, the people of Populism saw themselves. … In the world they created, they fulfilled the democratic promise in the only way it can be fulfilled – by people acting in democratic ways in their daily lives.[24]

For those seeking revolutionary change, these authors focus our attention on the critical importance of movement culture and the people's institutions that help to foster it between and through the "moment of the whirlwind."[25] Heterogeneous movements are more likely to innovate and succeed in winning critically important structural changes that will ultimately remake society, but they are not simply called into existence. When movement organizations realize the radical implications of a long-term agenda, then strategic alignment between social blocs becomes possible, and a heterogeneous movement may be born. Movement culture that directly confronts structural racism and other forms of structural oppression, which otherwise would limit the strength of these efforts, is a precondition for movements that seek to dismantle racial capitalism. As these authors have shown, strategic political education, deep and intensive training, intentional relationship building, and captivating campaigns are the crucibles of movement culture. These voices from the past are calling us to greatness if we choose to listen. Let's get to it. Ⓐ

Books Discussed

Engler, Mark, and Paul Engler, *This Is an Uprising: How Nonviolent Revolt is Shaping the Twenty-First Century*. New York: Bold Type Books, 2016.

brown, adrienne m. *Emergent Strategy: Shaping Change, Changing Worlds*. Chico, CA: AK Press, 2017.

Goodwyn, Lawrence. *The Populist Moment: A Short History of the Agrarian Revolt in America*. Abridged 1976 ed. Oxford: Oxford University Press, 1978.

Chenoweth, Erica, and Maria J. Stephan. *Why Civil Resistance Works: The Strategic Logic of Nonviolent Conflict*. New York: Columbia University Press, 2011.

James Mumm is an irrepressible organizer and aspiring writer. For the past three decades James has worked as an organizer in Chicago, the Bronx, New York, and nationally, investing in people-powered change with People's Action, Greenpeace USA, and local organizations. As a student of the game, James reads and writes about books that illuminate the path forward for transformational change. This essay is based on a previous version first published in Social Policy, Volume 49, Number 4 (Winter 2019).

Endnotes

1   Chenoweth, Erica, and Maria J. Stephan, *Why Civil Resistance Works: The Strategic Logic of Nonviolent Conflict* (New York: Columbia University Press, 2011), 13.

2   Chenoweth and Stephan, *Why Civil Resistance Works*, 6.

3   Chenoweth and Stephan, *Why Civil Resistance Works*, 7.

4   brown, adrienne m., *Emergent Strategy: Shaping Change, Changing Worlds* (Chico, CA: AK Press, 2017), 163.

5   Chenoweth and Stephan, *Why Civil Resistance Works*, 11.

6   brown, *Emergent Strategy*, 119.

7   Engler, M., & Engler, P, *This Is an Uprising: How Nonviolent Revolt is Shaping the Twenty-First Century* (New York: Bold Type Books, 2016), 27.

8   Goodwyn, Lawrence, *The Populist Moment: A Short History of the Agrarian Revolt in America*, Abridged 1976 ed. (Oxford: Oxford University Press, 1978), xviii.

9   Goodwyn, *The Populist Moment*, 295.

10 Engler and Engler, *This Is an Uprising*, 63.

11 Goodwyn, *The Populist Moment*, 296.

12 brown, *Emergent Strategy*, 1–2.

13 Chenoweth and Stephan, *Why Civil Resistance Works*, 56.

14 Chenoweth and Stephan, *Why Civil Resistance Works*, 11.

15 Engler and Engler, *This Is an Uprising*, 75.

16 Engler and Engler, *This Is an Uprising*, 76–77.

17 Goodwyn, *The Populist Moment*, 295.

18 Engler and Engler, *This Is an Uprising*, 145.

19 Goodwyn, *The Populist Moment*, xvii.

20 Goodwyn, *The Populist Moment*, 100.

21 Goodwyn, *The Populist Moment*, 122–123.

22 brown, *Emergent Strategy*, 52.

23 brown, *Emergent Strategy*, 15.

24 Goodwyn, *The Populist Moment*, 296.

25 Engler and Engler, *This Is an Uprising*, 54.

HYDROPOWER
A REVIEW BY MAIA RAMNATH

Undrowned by Alexis Pauline Gumbs (AK Press, 2020)
and *The Deep* by Rivers Solomon (Gallery/Saga Press, 2019)

IT BEGINS WITH BREATH.

That is, it begins with the planetary cycle of respiration connecting forest, ocean, air, and every creature.

Alexis Pauline Gumbs's *Undrowned: Black Feminist Lessons from Marine Mammals* is the invigorating second entry in adrienne maree brown's Emergent Strategy series with AK Press.

It's a set of nineteen meditations on themes inspired by aquatic animals as kindred souls, teachers, and mentors, demonstrating their marvelous knowledges and capabilities for navigating depth, pressure, turbulence, ice, storm, predation. Altogether our fellow mammals bring a wealth of "subversive and transformative guidance" (7) for *not* drowning in an environment that would steal breath – whether under water, or in a social reality brought into sharp focus this past year by both respiratory pandemic and the latest racist police violence.

These meditations are "thematic movements ... organized around core Black feminist practices like breathing, remembering, collaborating, etc.," (10) that open toward emergent, actionable insights. Each one weaves marine science, art, history, ethnology, politics, and mythology – especially from cultures most closely intertwined with the life of sea mammals – into what sounds as much like love songs as spiritual incantations. (The only other author that comes to mind who so deftly handles this many intricate threads is Rebecca Solnit.)

Undrowned is also a guidebook, but one that stands in stark contrast to those marine biology texts that offer their factual data in a neutral scientific tone while also projecting capitalist, colonialist, and patriarchal logics onto marine animals.

Taken instead on their own terms, belugas, narwhals, right whales, bowhead whales, riverine and oceanic dolphins, seals, sea lions, orcas, and manatees (plus the odd shark or manta ray) have much to teach: in navigating ice or sustaining breath in cold depths; shaping physicality to a fluid environment; the power of the dorsal fin (the bridge of the

back) for path making and stabilization; surviving captivity through community; surviving genocidal commodification of one's body under global capitalism; defying isolation by swimming in schools or pods; synchronizing movement as a model for large-scale direct action; "pantropical" multispecies marine clusters as analogs for collaboration in diasporic cooperatives; the fugitive advantages of hybridity (eluding domination and exceeding its categorizing knowledge); offering the wholeness of one's self while loving the whole of someone else, scars and all; and much much more.

What begins with respiration moves through inspiration to activation: the closing chapter offers suggestions for embodying the themes of each section, including appropriate variations for both Black and non-Black readers, in individual and "pod/squad" versions. "What are the intergenerational and evolutionary ways that we become what we practice?" prompts Gumbs. "How can we navigate oppressive environments with core practices that build community, resistance, and more loving ways of living?" (43).

What's more, Gumbs reminds readers that the waters in which marine mammals exist are a medium not only of breath, but of sound; in which echolocation – sending out signals, and even more importantly, listening for the pings back – places bodies in spatial relationship to their surroundings, structures, and other beings. "Some of this magic is just the complexity of being a mammal alive in sound. I can hear what I cannot see yet. I can make a whole world of resonance. And live in it. Swim through it. Reflecting you. Whistle, click if you can feel that I am here" (18).

Most fittingly then, each of the nineteen sections is planned to have its own musical counterpart by Toshi Reagon, to be released together as "Long Water Song."

Until that's available, there's always the Hugo-nominated song "The Deep" by the experimental hip-hop partnership Clipping (William Hutson, Jonathan Snipes, and Daveed Diggs), inspired in turn by the Afrofuturist mythology of 1990s electronic music duo Drexciya (James Stinson and Gerald Donald). Then read the speculative novella *The Deep* by Rivers Solomon, which reinterprets and expands the song into a new medium. This emergent body of collective work clearly exists within the same ecosystem as *Undrowned*.

Gumbs reminds us that the oceanic world through which her cetacean teachers move is also the world of the three-century-long brutality of the transatlantic slave trade, in which the millions who did not survive made a trail of graves below the water. Now imagine that the descendants of pregnant African women, kidnapped and thrown overboard from slave ships, were born into ocean, nurtured by cetacean "second mothers," then mutated and sea-changed into a submarine society of "strange fish" – the wajinru. Finned and gilled, they too exist in a medium of water-borne signals: sound, pressure, electricity.

In a culture based on the management of listening and remembrance, the ancestral memory of the wajinru foremothers is borne by one member, the historian of that generation, keeping the others shielded from the legacy of trauma except during a certain designated time of sharing. The ancestor who established this practice and relationship aimed to keep them safe from the pain, loneliness, abandonment, and fear that their forebears had known.

The burden takes its toll: historian Yetu is nearly broken by the weight of the memory she bears, drowning her individual selfhood. Fleeing the role and her people, she breaches the surface and battles the surf. On shore she encounters some "two-legs" – alien, yet distant kin – and forms a particular relationship with one, a tough mariner who feels another kind of fraught connection and fierce responsibility to a lost homeland across the sea.

Not all wajinru regard the two-legs as potential friends or allies: another historian unleashes titanic powers of storm and wave in anger at their oil drilling, exploitation, and despoliation of the depths. Perhaps the land mammals in question should be listening to Gumbs, learning from marine beings about "the vulnerability, collaboration, and adaptation we need in order to be with change at this time, especially since one of the major changes we are living through, causing, and shaping in this climate crisis is this rising of the ocean."

Yetu and her community need to renegotiate the balance between self and collective, past accountability and present agency, land and sea life, freedom to seek joy and love, and responsibility to bear witness to pain and hardship – neither being totally cut off from history nor being totally consumed by it is survivable. (For anarchists, what might also come to mind is the danger of centralizing too much knowledge and labor into the hands of too few, rather than decentralizing it and sharing access.)

So, why not suppose that amongst the whales, dolphins, and sharks of Gumbs's meditations might also exist wajinru, who have long been learning the lessons that she brings forth to the surface for us legged and lunged ones now: Listen. Breathe. Remember. Be vulnerable. Be present. Be fierce. Collaborate. Learn from conflict. Honor your boundaries. Go deep. Ⓐ

(Thank you, Chika, Libertie, Theresa, and Koala, for showing me cool stuff.)

Maia Ramnath is the author of Haj to Utopia: How the Ghadar Movement Charted Global Radicalism and Attempted to Overthrow the British Empire *(University of California Press, 2011) and* Decolonizing Anarchism: An Antiauthoritarian History of India's Liberation Struggle *(IAS/AK Press, 2012). She is a member of the* Perspectives *collective.*